Thunder, Flush
& Thomas Crapper

Thunder, Flush & Thomas Crapper

AN ENCYCLOOPEDIA

ADAM HART-DAVIS

THE
CHALFORD
PRESS

First published by Michael O'Mara Books in 1997
This edition published by The Chalford Press in 2008

The Chalford Press is an imprint of The History Press
Cirencester Road, Chalford, Stroud, Gloucestershire, GL6 8PE
www.thehistorypress.co.uk

British Library Cataloguing in Publication Data:
A catalogue record for this book is available from the British Library

ISBN 978 1 84588 609 7

Typesetting and origination by The History Press
Printed in Great Britain Ashford Colour Press

Contents

Preface

A few years ago I presented on television a short piece about Thomas Crapper. I enjoyed making it, but what amazed me was how much interest it generated; people are fascinated by lavatories. A friend, half-jokingly, said I should write a book about them, and I began to do some research. Again I was amazed, both by the sheer amount of fascinating material out there, and by people's enthusiasm. I have asked dozens of people for information and help; one or two ignored my requests, but the vast majority were much amused and keen to assist. Such grand organizations as the Regent's Park Zoo, The Royal Commission on the Historical Monuments of England, and the Ministry of Defence all had toilet tales to tell. Even the British Interplanetary Society, while regretting they 'do not have the first-hand information' nevertheless promised to try and get it.

We use lavatorial language all the time—yet we aren't allowed to talk about lavatories in public; there's a curious paradox here—*see* euphemisms. Lift the lid, though, and the stories are easy to flush out. That's why this book was such fun to write.

I have done my best to make sure that everything in the book is true. There are a few jokes and absurdities, but everything else is factual, I think, and I have checked what I could. If I have made mistakes I am sorry; please let me know if you find one.

People have told me wonderful stories of their experiences, from submarines to mountain tops. I have no way of checking these, and have had to accept them as they are. If any readers have wonderful stories to tell, please write to me c/o The Chalford Press—there might be another edition!

Finally, *How to use this book*. Either look up directly anything that interests you—royalty, perhaps, or Starship Enterprise, or open at random, and browse. Cross-references in the text refer to things directly related to what you have just been reading, and are shown either with a star, as in *cisterns, or by *see*; e.g. *see* trains.

The entries vary in length, and are designed to be easily readable while you are sitting on your loo ... I hope you enjoy them as much as I have.

Adam Hart-Davis
Bristol, January 1997

Acknowledgements

Many thanks to all these people and companies who have helped me: AMSTP, Armitage Shanks, Paul Bader, Martine and Stephen Batchelor, Dr David Bender, Paul Berriff, Biolet, Boeing, Audrey Booth, Dr Tony Boycott, Liz Brice, *Bristol Evening Post*, British Bathroom Council, British Rail, Gerry Brooke, Mike Burrows, Mrs J.F. Cameron, David Campbell, Castle Borders, Allan Chapman, Filip Cieslik, Clivus Multrum, Dr John Crook, Nick Davies, Dr Camilla Dixon, Margaret Drinkwater, Dr Martin Eastwood, Elsan, Ken English, English Heritage (Susie Barson and Frank Kelsall), Professor Ann Ferguson, Roger Ford, Jacqueline Fox, Professor Robert Freeman, Ken Gabrowski, Kelly Galpin, Diane Gascoyne, Dr Andy Gibbons, Bill Gibbs, Gladstone Pottery Museum, Dr Kate Gleeson, Gloucester Library, Nick Gray, R.B. Grinter, Michele Gunn, Geoffrey Hamer, Hanky Library, Dr W.S. Hanson, Melvin Harris, Damon Hart-Davis, Duff Hart-Davis, Guy Hart-Davis, Jason Hart-Davis, Sir Rupert Hart-Davis, B. Haynes, Dr Ken Heaton, John W. Hill, Charles Hirst, Honey Buckets, Hudson Memorial Library St Albans, Gwyn Hughes, Jamont, Lillian M. Jewkes, Jeyes, John Johnson Collection, Kylie Jones, Dr Peter Jones, Dr Andrew Jones, Dr Michael Kamm, Fred Karth, Gene Kennedy, Tamas Langley, Rachel Lea, Chris Ledger, Pippa Lewis, Nick Lodge, Victoria Logue, Nick Lord, Charles MacArthur, Ian MacFarlane, Mrs May Marks, Geof Martin, George Maycraft, Grant McKee,

D.J. Moloney, Bob Morrow, Catherine Mounsey, Frederic Mullally, National Monuments Accord, National Railway Museum (York), National Science Foundation (US), The National Trust, Mr J. Newby, Northumberland National Park, Jack Nutting, NWT Power Corporation, Jeffrey M. Oliver, Atsuko Oshima, P&O Ferries, Geoffrey Pidgeon, Ron Pilnick, Vincent Prosser, Janet Quarton, RADAR, RAMC Historical Museum, Margaret Reardon, Dr Bob Reed, Dr Matt Ridley, Simon Rose, Tom Rowley, The Royal Air Force, The Royal Navy, Jonathan Sanderson, Mike Sanderson, The Science Museum, Science Museum Library, Scott, Mike Shrimpton, Des Sleightholme, Doreen Smith, Dr Tony Smith, Star Trek Welcommittee, Rebecca Stephens, Belinda Stewart Cox, Ian Taylor, Thetford, Pat Thompson, Toto, Emily Troscianko, Jolyon Troscianko, Tom Troscianko, David W. Turner, Maryon Tysoe, Mrs Alice Varty, Nigel Vaulkhard, Dr Emma Walker, Roger Webb, Simon Welfare, Julia Wilkins, A. Winstanley, Dr Heinz Wolff, Women's Design Service, Sam Woodberry, and Mary Rose Young, but most of all my family for their patience, and the staff at the Cheltenham Road Library who were unfailingly helpful.

The publishers would like to thank the following for granting permission to reproduce illustrative material: Instrumental Furniture for the frontispiece; RAMC Historical Museum (p. 21); NASA (pp. 25 and 139); Jonathan Sanderson (p. 28): Jolyon Troscianko (pp. 39, 40 and 76); Dr Susan Blackmore (p. 41); Belinda Stewart Cox (p. 48); Fotomas (pp. 51 and 93); Centre for Alternative Technology (pp. 54, and 55); *Bristol Evening Post* (pp. 69 and 134); John Johnson Collection, Bodleian Library (pp. 71 and 73); Paula Cable (p. 76);

Kristina Ferris and Mike Scorer at *The Independent* (p. 91); Armitage Shanks (p. 96); Kjell Torstensson (pp. 99, 114, 131 and 132); Bob Olley (p. 100); Toto (p. 103); Jeyes (p. 105); Joan Harding at the Surrey Domestic Buildings Research Group (p. 110); Albert Weir (p. 113); Dorset County Museum (p. 117); Lynne McNab at Guild Hall Library (p. 123); Advertising Archive Limited (pp. 127 and 150); J.C. Decaux; (pp. 159 and 160); Peter Badcock (p. 162); © Studio Muller/News Productions (p. 164); Tamas Langley (p. 169); Mike Sandman (p. 172); Geoffrey Pidgeon (p. 180). The author supplied the original images for the illustrations on pp. 16, 24, 26, 32, 36, 47, 61, 69, 87, 89, 94, 137, 148, 153 and 166.

The publishers would also like to thank the following for granting permission to reproduce textual material: The Society of Authors as agents of the Strachey Trust for extract from Lytton Strachey, *Portraits in Miniature & Other Essays* (p. 88); Peters Fraser & Dunlop for extract from Evelyn Waugh, *Men at Arms* (p. 163).

Whilst every effort has been made to trace the owners of copyright material, in a few cases this has proved to be problematic and so we take this opportunity to offer our apologies to any copyright holders whose rights we may have unwittingly infringed.

A

Abbot of St Albans

The Abbey of St Albans was consecrated in AD 1115. The Abbot built a stone cistern to hold rainwater, which he used to flush his lavatory; so he may have been the first Englishman to have a *water-closet.

Acton Court

At Iron Acton near Bristol, the wonderful house of Acton Court was built around 1534 by Sir Nicholas Poyntz apparently especially for a royal visit; Henry VIII took Anne Boleyn there for the weekend.

The house is now being restored, and one of the major discoveries was the garderobe—just a crude hole in a cupboard (which appears to have been widened for the royal visitor)—with a 22 foot drop down a stone shaft into the moat.

Adamson, George

For 30 years, George Adamson, legendary lion-man of Africa and subject of the film *Born Free*, used a spectacular *privy at his camp at Kora Game Reserve in northern Kenya, right on the equator. It was used also by royalty both British and American (i.e. film stars), and by Nick Gray and Mike Shrimpton, who described it to me.

This two-seater, enclosed by matting walls, was natural, comfortable, and appropriate. The seats were upturned elephants' jaws on wooden frames, suspended above a trench. Paper was contained in a can to cheat the ants. A trowel was at hand to cover the deposit with sand before the whole contraption was moved along the ditch, ready for the next occupant(s).

When George Adamson was murdered by bandits in 1989, his camp was destroyed. Nothing now remains of the magnificent privy where George and his guests used to sit under the African sky.

Aerosols

Flushing a lavatory produces an aerosol—a fine mist of water particles—that can carry bacteria from the bowl and could lead to infection. Researchers deliberately contaminated the water in the pan with a bacterial culture, and showed that after flushing, bacteria were easily detectable at a point 40cm away and level with the edge of the seat.

They showed that a double-trap siphonic flush produced much less aerosol than a standard wash-down pan; bacteria were still detectable, but at a concentration 14 times lower; *see* siphonic action.

Surprisingly, however, they found that closing the lid on the wash-down pan failed to contain the bacteria; indeed it seemed to make the situation worse!

Aircraft

From the earliest days of flying, aircrew have needed methods of relieving themselves, and when passengers started paying fares they soon demanded lavatories. The problems are that flushing lavatories need space and water; space is always limited in aircraft, and water is heavy stuff to carry around.

Even in the 1930s, regulations laid down that no solid matter could be discharged in flight; the first aircraft lavatories were Elsans; *see* chemical lavatories, RAF aircrew.

Next came a closet with a valve, through which excrement fell into a tank in the floor, though the squirt flush could not cope with serious air-sickness. A jacketed pan with enough water for 30 flushes was a bit better, but the user had to tip the whole pan to flush and discharge the contents.

Finally Imperial Airways settled on a lavatory in which the waste was chemically sterilized, the solids filtered out, and the sterile liquid recirculated by force-pump. This provided an unlimited number of satisfactory flushes without a heavy weight of water.

Boeing

The Boeings 727 and 737 boasted two or three loos, each an independent recycling unit with an integral waste tank. They were primed with three gallons of water and a concentrated solution of disinfectant, deodorant, and dye. Flushing pumped two gallons of liquid during 10 seconds into a rotating filter and into the bowl. The outflow went into a 17-gallon fibreglass tank, and the liquid was recirculated.

On the ground, the contents of the tanks were removed through a four-inch drain outlet in the toilet service panel into ground service carts, known as honey carts. If a pump failed, the lavatory could still be used as a simple chemical lavatory.

When they introduced the 767 in 1982, Boeing unveiled a vacuum-waste system, which had taken more than ten years of research and development, and has been used on most new aircraft since then. All the lavatories in the aircraft are connected to two large central waste tanks by two-inch pipes. When you press

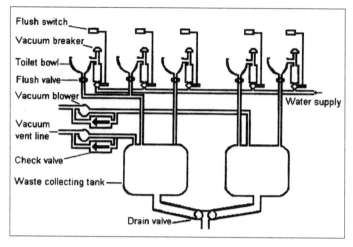

Aircraft vacuum waste system

the flush control, water is released for a few seconds into the bowl, then the inlet valve at the top of the bowl closes and the outlet valve at the bottom opens, and the entire contents of the bowl are sucked down into the holding tanks. The bowl empties in just four seconds, after which the valve closes again, leaving a clean dry bowl for the next user.

On the ground and immediately after take-off the vacuum is generated by a fan, but once the aircraft has reached 16,000 feet, the difference between cabin pressure and outside air pressure provides all the vacuum needed.

The main advantages of this system are that all the waste can be collected by the honey carts from one or two outlets, and the lavatories are less smelly because the waste is kept elsewhere.

The primary disinfectant used to be formaldehyde, but now a secret 'green' compound is used. It is added in the form of sachets to the flushing water.

Green ice
Despite all the regulations, and the precautions taken by the airlines, there are persistent rumours about airplane toilets which have leaked through to the outside of the plane. At high altitudes the air is extremely cold, so everything freezes on the outside of the plane; ice accumulates until the chunks are heavy enough to drop off. In Denver, Colorado there are frequently reported stories of lumps of 'green ice' on housewives' lawns.

On 7 March 1976 W. W. 'Comet' Cullers was watching the six-million-dollar man on television in his home in Timberville, Virginia. Suddenly, with a colossal roar, a lump of ice the size of a basketball crashed through his roof on to the living-room rug between his feet and the television set. He called the police, and Sergeant Butch Hottinger of the Rockingham County Sheriff's Department investigated the case thoroughly, but was unable to account for the ice.

Such ice-falls have been reported hundreds of times. Perhaps they do come from aircraft, but are simply accumulations of snow or rainwater, frozen at high altitude, rather than leaks from lavatories.

Under pressure
Another often-repeated story tells of a very large woman relieving herself in the loo, completely covering the rim. The plane was lurching uncomfortably, and she was nervous, so she flushed it without getting up. Because of the suction she was pulled down into the bowl, and suffered discomfort and perhaps some injury. She could not be released until air had been pumped into the system.

Boeing say this cannot happen during normal flight. Not only is the flush control behind the seat, so that to operate the flush while sitting on the bowl with the seat up is extremely difficult, but they claim the pressure difference is too low to trap anyone. Theoretically there is enough pressure difference during take-off, but then the seat-belt signs are on, and passengers are not allowed into the toilets.

See also boats.

Amerdale House

Situated on the edge of the village of Arncliffe, in the heart of the Yorkshire Dales, this hotel boasts a magnificent boxed-in *wash-down closet made by Gratrix of Manchester; a veritable throne, definitely *vaut le détour*. The proprietors are Nigel and Paula Crapper, but they are not related to Thomas *Crapper!

Army

Victorian

The manual for the Medical Staff Corps of 1894 has just four paragraphs on latrines:

> Latrines should be made as soon as the troops arrive on the ground.
>
> A small shallow trench will suffice for one night, and should be invariably filled in in the morning, before the troops march off. In standing camps latrines may be made with seats, as shown ...
>
> The seat being a simple rough pole, the trench should be made as narrow as possible, and from three to four feet deep. A fatigue party should throw a couple of inches of earth over the soil every day. This, if carefully done, will prevent all smell.
>
> In a standing camp urinals should be established.

Edwardian

The Royal Army Medical Corps Training Manual of 1911, para. 134, is more explicit, and has eight pages of detailed instructions: 'The moment a camp or bivouac is about to be formed or occupied the first duty of the commanding officer is ... the location and preparation of latrines and urinals. The construction of these necessaries must not be delayed until the tents are pitched ... no matter how temporary the halt may be, the location and completion of these places is an urgent necessity ...'

Para. 135 provides the details: 'The general location of latrines will depend on the direction of the prevailing wind ... the rule being to place them to leeward of the camp and in such a position that no possible fouling of the water supply can result. ... Latrines and urinals should be as far removed from the camp as is compatible with convenience; under ordinary circumstances this may be put at 100 yards.'

1930s

The 1934 Army Manual of Hygiene and Sanitation takes the subject even more seriously, and devotes the whole of Chapter VIII—16 pages—to Field sanitary appliances. Despite the jargon, the instructions come through clearly.

Three types of latrine are in common use in the field:
1. The shallow trench latrine.
2. The deep trench latrine.
3. The bucket latrine.

1. The shallow trench latrine is not satisfactory and should only be used for short halts ... The trenches are

dug in rows allowing 5 for the first 100 men and 3 for
every additional 100. Each trench should be 3 feet long,
1 foot wide, and 2 feet deep ...

The principle is neat; the excavated earth is piled behind
the trench; the men squat astride it, and after each has
finished he uses a little earth to cover his excrement with a
scoop or spade. After 24 hours the trenches are filled in.

Never let it be said that the army is resistant to change.
Just look at this amazing U-turn:

2. Deep trench latrine. The old type of deep pit latrine,
with a pole across to sit on, should never be used, as it
is conducive to fouling the sides of the trench ... flies ...
disease ... The fly-proof deep trench latrine is a good
type and should be used in all camps of four or more
days' duration ...

There follow detailed instructions for the digging of
trenches 6 to 8 feet deep, 3 feet wide, and 10 feet long,
to accommodate the first 100 men.

The bucket latrines for billeting areas and railway
stations needed much less hard work. What's more,
with five buckets per hundred men 'with extra ones for
serjeants', and fly-proof self-closing lids, they sound
like far better facilities than were offered by the railway
companies at the time!

There is information on latrines for Indian troops—
squatters who 'do not use latrine paper'—on the 'abdast'
or washing platform for those who cleanse themselves
with water, and on Otway's pit, which is a type of cesspool.
There is also a slightly disturbing requirement for 'close
supervision by the regimental sanitary police ...'

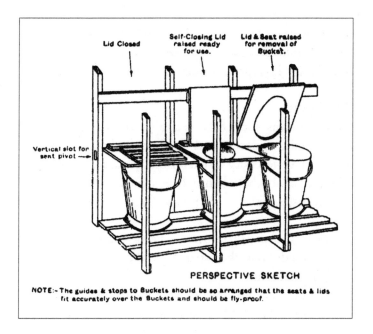

PERSPECTIVE SKETCH

NOTE:- The guides & stops to Buckets should be so arranged that the seats & lids fit accurately over the Buckets and should be fly-proof.

Army exams

An incompetent officer cadet boasted he could answer every question in an army exam, and still score zero. He did not read the questions, but simply wrote 'Dig lats' for every answer. Unfortunately question 17 was 'What is the first thing to do on setting up a new camp?' So he scored one mark.

For the latest regulations, *see* NATO.

Astronauts

The first person to be rocketed into space, on 12 April 1961, was the 27-year-old Russian test-pilot Yuri Gagarin. He became an international hero, but his lavatorial facilities were probably minimal, since his flight lasted only just long enough to complete one orbit of the Earth.

Three weeks later, on 5 May 1961, the first American, Alan Sheppard, went into space—and it was the occasion of an acute lavatorial problem; *see* right stuff.

The 1960s

Sheppard was soon followed by further Mercury and then Gemini missions, and the space flights began to last longer. The necessity of excretion could not be ignored. The human body, when active, needs to excrete every few hours; some way had to be found to get rid of the effluent.

Three separate problems of 'waste management' had to be solved. First, the astronauts were encased in tough airtight spacesuits.

Second, their movements were highly restricted. They could move their limbs a few inches each way, but there was no possibility of turning round, let alone going to another part of the spacecraft—there was no other part of the spacecraft. So some sort of container had to be devised to hold the urine.

Third, zero gravity. Even if a male astronaut had a vent in his suit through which he could reach his penis, and could move his arms enough to bring up a bottle, he could not pee into it, for in the weightlessness of space there is no such thing as 'down', and the liquid would just bounce out of the bottle and spray all over the spacecraft. For a woman the difficulties would be greater. This problem was raised in the film *2001, A Space Odyssey*; *see* zero-gravity toilet.

These three problems were so tough that in the early days NASA chose a simple if inelegant solution; the astronauts wore absorbent underwear like diapers, or nappies! With elephantine euphemism, these were called 'intimate-contact devices'. Urine was collected inside the spacesuits with a 'roll-on cuff and bag system'; faeces by 'absorbent diaper-type underwear and a stick-on colostomy bag'. These methods were claimed to be functional, although they were difficult to use, time-consuming, and messy.

The 1970s

By the end of the 1960s missions were lasting several days, and better solutions had to be found. The spacecraft cabin was normally pressurized, so the astronauts did not have to be sealed into spacesuits; they took to wearing shorts and t-shirts. Eventually a 'waste collection system'—WCS—was designed for use by both men and women.

One thing they did have was a vacuum—since space itself is a vacuum. So they urinated into the soft triangular nozzle of a sort of vacuum cleaner, which removed the liquid and squirted it out into space. This sounded fine, but in practice the vacuum was not quite strong enough, and whoever went to use the nozzle found it still wet from the last person.

There was also the slight problem that the urine tended to hang around the ship and travel along with it as a cloud of ice particles.

The 1990s

Tremendous efforts—and $30 million—were expended to improve the loo for the EDO (extended duration orbiter) missions in the 1990s.

The new urinal can be used either standing or sitting. Beyond the nozzle, the urine passes through a pre-filter to collect hair, and then into a fan separator. This rotates at 3,900 rpm, and pumps the urine out sideways by centrifugal action. The air goes through the centre of this fan, through a filter to remove smell and bacteria, and

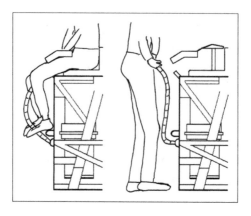

back to the cabin. The urine is collected in a pressurized waste tank.

The airflow is provided by a separate fan, rotating at 14,000 rpm. This is a big improvement on the old system, which had only one fan. The problem of the wet nozzle is at least partly solved by this extra fan, and by the fact that it continues to run for 60 seconds after the user has restored the urinal hose to its stowed position, ready for the next person.

Using the WCS

To sit on the loo, the astronaut opens the WCS compartment door, extends the privacy curtains, and manoeuvres on to the seat with thighs under the bars and feet in foot restraints—since this is one place you do not want to float away from in zero gravity! The Skylab WCS (*see opposite*) used a waist belt and handholds, but thigh restraints were thought to be better.

Push forward the operating handle on the right to focus 11 jets of air inwards at the point just below your anus where the 'bolus' (i.e. faeces) will emerge, which has the effect of actually pulling it away. On earlier

missions, astronauts had found that without help from gravity the faeces stuck to their bottoms. The air-jets help, but unfortunately they tend to be icy cold.

Skylab
In the Skylab WCS the faeces were pulled into a 'slinger', which worked like a top-loading spin-drier. Vanes spinning at 1,500 rpm shredded the solid and spun it out to the wall of the drum, where it was deposited as a thin layer. This gradually dried out, since closing the lid also opened the vent valve, exposing the drum to the vacuum of space. This worked, slightly too well.

After a few days small pieces of dry solid began to flake off, and some escaped into the cabin. This would not have mattered, except that the astronauts could not resist flicking their weightless food about, and the time came when they could not tell the difference between a floating peanut and a floating piece of dried excrement, except by the taste.

There were other problems. The excrement tended to build up unevenly in the drum; so every day one member of the crew had to put on a rubber glove and spread it around so that it would not block the system. And each astronaut was allowed to use only one sheet of paper, for fear of preventing the drying process.

Space loos today

These problems have now been solved by containing the faeces in collection bags like those in vacuum cleaners; they collect all the solid and liquid, and allow the air to pass through. A new bag is in place when you sit on the WCS. When you have finished, the compactor squashes the bag to the bottom of the collection canister and compresses it. Then you push the compactor back to its stored position, put in a new bag for the next person, and close the seat and lid, which switches off the air blower.

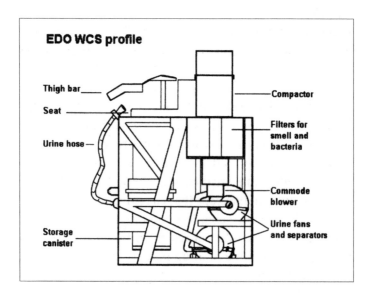

In order to minimize the amount of excrement to dispose of, astronauts are normally given a zero-fibre diet, since the weight of faeces depends on the amount of fibre in the food. Furthermore, at least one astronaut was so nauseated by the lavatory that he refused to eat anything at all for the four days of his mission.

The Russian system
In their Mir spacecraft, the Russians have more experience of long missions, and they were amused to discover the expensive new NASA loos were just like their well-tried ones, although trickier to use. The Russian urinal has separate nozzles—round for men and triangular for women, with a simple screw fitting. They wipe round the nozzle to dry it after use.

Cosmonauts use both wet and dry wipes to clean themselves, and eat plenty of fibre to keep their intestinal muscles working.

Australia
Australians have a number of expressions for the lavatory, including 'thunder-box', but the standard word is 'dunny', and the paper is called a 'dunny-roll'. They may say they want to 'go down the garden', 'go to the library', 'go out back', or 'go to the outback'.

A slightly ancient expression was 'the proverbial brick shithouse', sometimes shortened to 'proverbial', as in a story recounted by Wallace Reyburn. A man he knew went into a pub in Australia and found an open gutter running along the front of the actual bar, two or three feet off the ground, with urine trickling down it. The bartender said that before he put it up he lost a lot of money because the men had to waste so much valuable drinking time going outside to the proverbial.

Australian privies used to have cut-up newspaper for wiping, and a potential hazard in the form of red-back spiders.

Austria

At Innsbruck AlpenZoo in 1995, Jonathan Sanderson discovered a 'CWS Cleanseat' lavatory (*see below*). As it flushes, a door in the cistern flips open, and a little arm reaches out and attaches itself to the seat, which then rotates while being scrubbed. This looks good, but the seat remains imperfectly clean.

I remember from the 1950s a story about a British couple who wanted to stay in a small hotel in Austria, but were worried about the plumbing; so they wrote a letter to the proprietor and asked about the WC. Not being good at English, he went for advice to the local priest, who told him that WC was short for Wesleyan Chapel. So he wrote back 'The WC is situated in a beautiful position only three miles from our door. There is seating for 75 persons, and the acoustics are superb …' I have heard many versions of this story over the years, but for some reason it is always about Austria. Perhaps it really happened once?

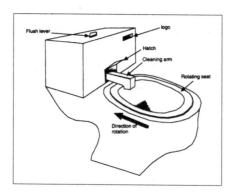

B

Ballcock

The ballcock is the floating ball on a hinged arm that controls the water level in the lavatory *cistern.

After flushing, the cistern is empty, and the ball hangs down. The inlet valve is open, and water runs in. As the cistern fills, the floating ball lifts its arm until the inlet valve closes and stops the flow of water.

Bible

Saul

The Authorized (King James) Version of the Bible is full of blood and lust, but rather coy about lavatories. The best known verse is 1 Samuel 24:3:

> And he came to the sheepcotes by the way, where there was a cave; and Saul went in to cover his feet ...

The Hebrews generally wore short tunics, which would cover their feet only when they squatted. However, this interpretation may be too literal as there is evidence to suggest that 'feet' were a euphemism for genitals; so Saul went into the cave to hide his genitals (either from God or from the others). We can still assume that he really wanted to do a number two. A Latin version goes 'Spelunca quam ingresses est Saul, ut purgaret ventrem'; which means roughly 'Saul went into a cave to defecate'. The New English Bible says 'Saul came to the cave, and went in to relieve himself'.

The New American Bible (1970) translates this as '... he entered to ease nature'. The New Revised Standard Version (USA, 1989) has '... Saul went in to relieve himself'. However, one American version gave '... and Saul went to the bathroom'. As a result this became known as 'The Bathroom Bible'.

The murder of Moab

The same foot-covering euphemism is used in the middle of a lurid assassination story, in which Ehud kills Eglon, King of Moab (Judges 3:24): 'When he was gone out, his servants came; and when they saw that, behold, the doors of the parlour were locked, they said, Surely he covereth his feet in his summer chamber.' The New English Bible says 'He must be relieving himself in the closet of his summer palace.' Only later do the servants break in, and find the poor chap has been murdered.

Jehu

In 2 Kings 10:27 Jehu's men 'brake down the house of Baal, and made it a draught house ...'—or in the NEB 'pulled down ... the temple ... and made a privy of it'.

The draught

In the New Testament also the word draught is used to mean drain or privy, as in Matthew 17:17 'Do not ye yet understand, that whatsoever entereth in at the mouth goeth into the belly, and is cast out into the draught?'

And similarly in Mark 8:18, 19 'Do ye not perceive, that whatsoever thing from without entereth into the man, it cannot defile him; Because it entereth not into his heart, but into the belly, and goeth out into the draught?'

Bioloos

Both faeces and urine contain useful materials that can in principle be used for fertilizer. The problems are that they are smelly, and faeces contain dangerous pathogens that can cause disease. Most people flush the whole lot into sewers, and hand the problems to the sewage farms. Others take a more environmentally-friendly approach.

One way to overcome the problem of the pathogens is to make sure the sewage is digested thoroughly and aerobically by bacteria. This can be done passively—*see* composting lavatories—or actively in bioloos.

The domestic bioloo

The domestic bioloo is essentially a plastic box with a lavatory seat and lid on top. Inside is developing compost, but this is hidden under a cover, which opens automatically when you sit down. Mains electricity is used to warm air and pull it through the compost.

In a compost heap, and on the forest floor, bacteria break down plant matter into compost or humus. The idea of the bioloo is to provide the environment in which the same happens to sewage—which is also largely dead plant matter.

Each time you use the lavatory, you mix the contents of the box, either by turning a handle on top or with an electric motor. This frequent mixing of the contents, coupled with warmth and forced aeration, ensures that digestion is aerobic and efficient. Air is pulled down through the lavatory seat and under the compost, and then pushed out through a vent pipe in the roof. This airflow removes all the smell, and also evaporates most of the water. Since even faeces are up to 90% water, the sewage is reduced to one tenth of its original volume.

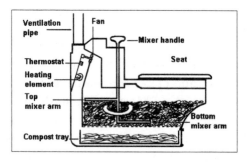

The advantages claimed for such systems are that they need no mains water, no chemicals, and no drains or septic tank. They cannot freeze in winter; they are smell- and trouble-free, they provide some useful compost for the garden, and the seat is always warm.

The Biolet Automatic

A standard unit, such as the Biolet Automatic, will cope with between four and six people using the house as a holiday cottage, and will need emptying only once a year. For everyday use in a permanent home, it will need emptying more often—perhaps even once a week—but then that is claimed to be easy. Just pull out the drawer, and dig the contents into the garden. And when you go away, pull out the plug, or it may dry right out.

The main disadvantage of bioloos is that they need electricity, and use it all the time they are plugged in. I understand they use roughly the same amount of electricity as a fridge, or perhaps a bit more. There are non-electric versions, but they are essentially just composting lavatories.

Bioloos have been used at the base camp of the British Antarctica Expedition, and by the Forestry Commission, British Rail, the Royal Navy, and the National Trust.

See also earth-closets, eco-loos, Royal Navy.

Blandford House

Right in the middle of Newcastle-upon-Tyne, Blandford House is now a museum, but in the 1930s it was the headquarters of the CWS, and a palatial art-deco lavatorial suite was built for the directors. Visit the Tyne and Wear Archives Department, and you too can revel in the luxury of polished wood, blue tiles, gold leaf, and stained glass.

Boats

Those caught short in a dinghy, canoe, or other small boat, have a tricky problem. Men can pee overboard— downwind, if possible. Otherwise the best solution is to use a bucket—or the baler—and empty it overboard. This is known as the 'bucket and chuck it' system. *See also* funnels.

On larger boats men can still pee over the side, preferably looping an arm round a stay; then you have both hands free and cannot go overboard. At anchor, tradition is to pee over the stern.

Most boats with cabins have some sort of on-board lavatory, which has to solve two problems: first, unless there is a large undesirable holding tank, any water-closet must discharge into the water outside; but once there is a hole in the hull, water might potentially come in and sink the boat. Second, boats can't carry unlimited quantities of fresh water, and using sea water for flushing causes corrosion of valves and stopcocks.

Small freshwater craft such as narrow boats on canals generally rely on *chemical lavatories, since they cannot discharge sewage into the water, but have access to sewage facilities on land.

Larger boats, such as cross-channel ferries, usually have vacuum systems. These empty the loo with suction, and then refill the trap and bowl with a small quantity (0.4 litres) of fresh water. The sewage is transferred to a treatment plant, aerated and chlorinated on board, and then pumped overboard. *See* aircraft, which use a similar system. These lavatories can trap the unwary; in 1986 an American woman flushed one while sitting on it in a cruise ship called *Pegasus* anchored off Vancouver, and sustained serious injuries. Apparently her buttocks and thighs completely covered the top of the bowl, and she received the full force caused by the pressure difference generated by the vacuum system.

Glass loos

The container ships owned by the German company Hapag Lloyd were fitted with glass lavatories on the bridge—the pilot had a panoramic view to port and starboard even while enthroned—so that the crew for a 30,000-tonne ship could be cut to 13 members.

See also submariners, Royal Navy, yachts.

Bottom of the world

Extreme cold produces several lavatorial problems. First, water is not generally available, because it is frozen. Second, sewage pipes cannot be laid underground, and would anyway freeze up; waste has to be removed in some other way. Third, bacteria are inactive at low temperatures; so sewage does not decay, but just sits there, fouling the environment.

The South Pole

There is a permanent American scientific research post at the South Pole, which has as many as 100 visiting scientists during the brief three-month summer around Christmas, but after the last plane leaves in mid-February becomes home to only about 28 hardy volunteers, who apart from the world-wide-web are cut off for nine months.

They use conventional lavatories, but with two modifications. They get their water by a cunning device called a Rodriguez Well. Hot water is pumped continuously down into the ice in small quantities, and this allows a large amount of cold water to be drawn off as the ice melts around the pipe.

Liquid waste is piped into sewage flumes under the top layer of ice. All solid waste is collected, flown to McMurdo Base in the spring, and then shipped out by sea during the summer months.

British Antarctic bases have *bioloos.

Packing it out
Rebecca Stephens reports that on a mountaineering expedition in Antarctica they were required to collect and remove all their waste. So they peed into a barrel, and defecated into black plastic bags. This was only slightly awkward, but the sledge with the plastic bags did get unpleasantly smelly in the sunshine, and towing it over the ice was not her favourite job!

See also igloos, SAS.

Bramah, Joseph
Joseph Bramah was a brilliant engineer, who invented a lavatory, a lock, and the beer engine, not to mention the hydraulic press.

Born in a farmhouse near Barnsley in Yorkshire in 1748, he would probably have stayed on the farm, but an accident in his youth prevented this, and he became apprenticed to a cabinet-maker. Told to fit a new water-closet, he was struck by its poor design, and in 1778 patented a new one.

The Bramah closet was similar to *Cumming's, but had a hinged valve under the pan instead of a sliding valve, which meant it was less liable to become encrusted and to freeze up, and so it leaked less.

The Bramah had a couple of clever refinements. Pulling the handle to open the valve and let out the excrement also turned on the water to flush the pan. Pushing it down again closed the valve and activated a neat delaying mechanism in the shape of a brass air-cylinder, which kept water running into the pan for about 15 seconds, so as to fill it ready for the next user.

Bramah closets still tended to leak a bit, since valves permanently under water will leak in the end. And they had another drawback; the complexity of the mechanism meant that they were liable to go wrong. Nevertheless, they were beautifully made; within 20 years he claimed he had sold 6,000, and for 100 years they remained the best lavatories in the land.

Britannia

Rumour has it that when the Royal Yacht *Britannia* was taken into dock for a refit, the mahogany lavatory seats were all removed and replaced. Allegedly, the wood from the old ones was not thrown away, but elegantly fashioned by a dockyard carpenter into presentation cigarette boxes. The owners of these boxes still lovingly stroke the seasoned wood, and wonder which of the noblest and barest royal bottoms had been there before.

British Standards

BS6465, Part 1 (1984) provides a scale of the minimum requirements in the provision of sanitary appliances in cinemas, concert halls, and so on:

Appliances	For male public	For female public
	In theatres, concert halls, and similar premises	
WCs	Min 1 for up to 250 males plus 1 for every additional 500	Min 2 for up to 50 females. 3 for 51 to 100, plus 1 for every additional 40.
Urinals	Min 2 for up to 100 males plus 1 for every additional 80.	

In cinemas

WCs	Min 1 for up to 100 males	Min 2 for up to 75 females.
	plus 1 for every additional	3 for 76 to 150, plus one for
	80.	every additional 80.
Urinals	Min 2 for up to 200 males	
	plus 1 for every additional 100.	

Why the requirements should differ for theatres and for cinemas is not clear; 200 men in a theatre apparently need one WC and four urinals, but if a film is shown there they suddenly need three WCs and only two urinals!

Building regulations

Approved Document G of the *Building Regulations 1991* published by the Department of the Environment and the Welsh Office (1992 edition) requires that any dwelling-house must have at least one lavatory and one wash-basin.

Any room containing a lavatory or urinal must be separated by a door from a space used for the preparation of food or for washing up.

Wash-basins should be in the same room as the closet or in the next room—provided it is not used for preparing food—and must have both hot and cold water.

Bumf

'Bumf' (or 'bumph') is a rude word for paper or papers, and is short for 'bum-fodder'; i.e. lavatory paper. *See also* Latin literature, paper.

C

Cars

Former pub landlord Cliff Conway from Bournemouth invented a car-loo, using vacuum-sealed plastic sachets that could be emptied out, disinfected, and used again. *See* pee-bottles.

Castles

Castles were built to last, and many survive from the Middle Ages to this day. Since the defenders had to be able to live in them, they all had some form of lavatory. The most common type was called a garderobe, originally a French word meaning wardrobe—a place to keep clothes in. (Today we still sometimes use the word 'cloakroom' to mean lavatory!)

The typical garderobe was an opening like a cupboard built into the thickness of the castle wall, high up near

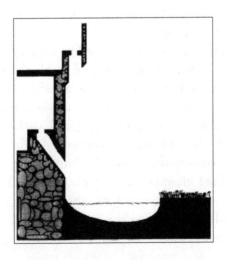

or on the battlements. There was a seat with a hole in it, and below that a chute leading diagonally out through the wall, so that the excrement fell into the moat or river or into a pit below.

Sometimes a buttress would contain a single garderobe; other castles boasted a block of two or three on each floor, above one another, with many shafts. There were four seats on each of three floors in the privy tower at Langley Castle in Northumberland, built in the late fourteenth century. At the Tower of London, conveniently near the banqueting hall, is a small vaulted chamber with a narrow window, and a short shaft that discharged into the moat.

Disposal straight into the moat efficiently removed the excrement outside the walls. What's more, when the drawbridge was raised, invading troops would have to cross the moat to reach the bottom of the castle wall. Swimming through water would have been bad enough, wearing a suit of armour, but wallowing through a cesspit must have required motivation above and beyond the normal call of duty.

One problem with this type of garderobe was that the chute had to be angled; so sticky excrement must often have stuck to the sides, creating foul smells, especially in warm weather. Usually there was no flushing system, although at Warkworth Castle— Harry Hotspur's pad—there is a broad shaft which both lets light in and acts as a funnel for rainwater. This could be directed into a tank at the bottom, but was normally piped along to flush out the discharge shafts from the latrines.

Another problem was that the chute provided a hole in the defences, and several castles were taken after

intrepid invaders climbed up the garderobe chutes. One neat solution was to make the garderobes stick straight out from the walls (corbelled), so that the waste dropped straight from the hole into the moat.

Below the garderobe hole at Castle Stalker near Fort William is a drop of 100 feet into the sea—a tough climb for invaders. Alas, to use it you have to turn your back on the magnificent sea view, and in a westerly gale, the wind comes straight up the hole, so lowering yourself onto the seat is not easy!

Chamber-pots

Picture the scene in the middle of the night 200 years ago. It's dark, and raining, and your bladder is full. There is no lavatory in the house, and the privy is at the other end of the back-yard. You do not want to go out in the rain. For the night everyone had a chamber-pot; it was often called a 'gozunder' because it goes under the bed.

Except for emergencies, pots were used only for urine; faeces smell much worse, and were harder to clean up.

Today bed-pans and urinals are still useful for people who are bedridden, so they are common in hospitals; but in the past they were everywhere.

Ancient Greece

Chamber-pots have been used for thousands of years. In the fifth century BC the Greek writer Aeschylus wrote in a play that pots were mirth-provoking missiles. In his play *The Clouds*, Aristophanes wrote of Socrates throwing his chamber-pot out of the window. Some Greek writers claimed that chamber-pots were invented by the Sybarites in southern Italy, but there seems no reason why they should really have been the first.

Ancient Rome
In AD 79 the Roman emperor *Vespasian was sitting on his pot when he felt the approach of death. His final words were said to be 'Vat, Auto, deus fio' which means 'I think I am becoming a god'.

The Middle Ages
In medieval times pots were called 'originals', and were often made of glass or glazed pottery, with a narrow neck and a wide mouth like a funnel. This meant the user could pee into it without having to get out of a warm bed. Also, glass pots allowed doctors to inspect the urine for diagnosis; *see* urinals.

By the fourteenth century chamber-pots were being made of tin, pewter, copper, and even gold. They were common objects, and not usually hidden. What's more,

pots were so convenient they were kept in other rooms also; often in cupboards in the dining-room sideboard, for example. *Close stools were often just pots in boxes, and pots with seats and lids found their way into carriages and trains.

The eighteenth century

In the 1720s Edward Burt, travelling in the Scottish highlands, wrote in a letter that he got up early from his bed-box at an inn, and 'unluckily set my foot in the chamber-pot'.

During the eighteenth century the craftsmen of North Staffordshire perfected the art of making china white throughout its thickness, and began to make beautiful chamber-pots, smooth and easy to clean. This part of the country came to be called The Potteries. Pots were printed on and otherwise decorated; noble families had coats of arms; ordinary folk had jokes.

Some pots had in the bottom portraits of national villains. An early target was Dr Henry Sacheverell (1674–1724), radical preacher and politician, once described as bold, insolent, passionate, and inordinately vain. In Clapton a manufacturer of pots featuring Sacheverell's face made a fortune and built himself a grand house, which was locally called Piss-Pot Hall. Other well-loved targets were Napoleon, and much later Adolf Hitler.

The nineteenth century

Many pots were printed with jokes and rude rhymes; a long-lasting favourite was a picture of a giant eye looking up from the bottom, with the legend:

Use me well, and keep me clean
And I'll not tell what I have seen.

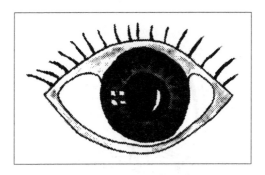

Sometimes they were rigged to play tricks; one nineteenth-century pot had a hidden musical box that played a tune when the pot was lifted, and could not be turned off.

Chemical lavatories

In 1924 Mr E.L. Jackson invented a device that was basically a bucket containing chemicals to kill bacteria in faeces and quell the smell of urine. He called his company ELSAN, from EL (his initials) and SANitation. The word Elsan is now in the dictionary as a general name for a chemical lavatory.

The Elsan company provided lavatories for the earliest commercial aircraft, and to Bomber Command. They still supply lavatories for boats, caravans, coaches, aircraft and building sites.

The basic product is a blue-coloured 12% solution of formaldehyde in water. This kills bacteria; it is the same as formalin, used to preserve biological specimens. Its smell is not pleasant but is not as bad as raw sewage. However, formaldehyde is reckoned to be unfriendly to the environment; so Elsan now sell a green product (literally—it is coloured green) which contains a secret new bactericide but no formaldehyde.

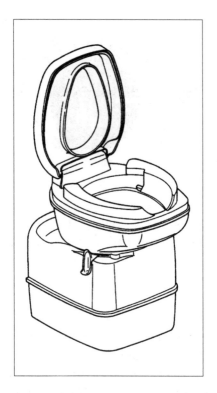

Elsan traditional lavatories, in three different models, are still essentially buckets with normal lavatory seats and lids. Newer models have a flushing pump and a sliding valve under the bowl. The waste tank underneath can be removed and carried like a suitcase for emptying.

The best-known American outfit is Honey Buckets, of Puyallup, Washington State.

See also bioloos, composting lavatories, eco-loos.

China
In rural China, the most common lavatory is a brick outhouse with a concrete floor. In the middle of the floor is a hole to squat over, without seat or bowl.

The excrement often falls on to a ramp that slopes down either into a field, from where it is collected for immediate use as fertilizer, or into a pig-pen; *see* pigs.

These simple privies are invariably smelly and unpleasant, yet people often take in books to read. Occasionally a privy serves only one house. Some are shared between two. More commonly there are only one or two for a whole village, in which case they are generally multi-holers.

The smell assaults you before you go in through the door; the building has two entrances, one for men and one for women. The rooms are divided by a thin and far-from-soundproof wall above a trench, a metre wide, which is the sewer. In each room there are between four and six open concrete chutes which slope down into it at 45°.

When the faeces finally reach the trench, millions of writhing white maggots mix them into the seething soup. This soup is filtered into another trench, and farmers come with buckets on yokes and carry it to their fields, where they pour it directly onto the crops, including

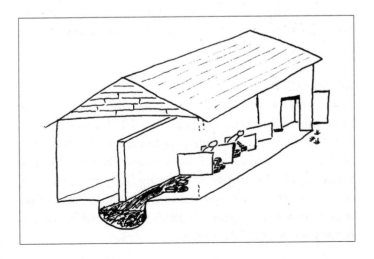

vegetables. In the late 1950s more than 90% of human excrement went on the fields, and made up one third of all the fertilizer that was used.

In large towns and cities, teams of two or three people known as 'honey-dippers' wheeled round a long round barrel on wheels, like a small milk lorry, collecting the effluent from communal lavatories and taking it to a common septic tank.

Modern China

Now, modernization is sweeping the country; the government announced in October 1995 a public toilet revolution, as 'a sign that people's level of civilization is rising', according to Lou Xiaoqi. Thirty-eight new model public lavatories were being built, with running water and sewers. However, one critic said the budget was so low that upgrading all the 7,000 public loos in Beijing would take 125 years.

Split pants
Chinese toddlers don't have nappies; they usually wear split pants, and from the age of 10 or 11 months they pee on command. Mum holds the toddler up so that its bottom is underneath, with the split open, and the urine simply goes on the ground, without wetting the baby's clothes.

Cisterns
The cistern is the tank of water used for flushing the lavatory. Victorian plumbers liked to put the cistern high on the wall to provide a good head of water for a vigorous flush (*see below*). Modern 'close-coupled' or 'low-flush' lavatories have the cistern immediately behind and just above the bowl.

Automatic disinfecting closet

British Standard No. 7357 (1990) demands that cisterns should have float-operated inlet valves, and covers. When tested, low-level cisterns must discharge between 6.5 and 7.5 litres of water at a minimum rate of 1.6 litres per second; high-level ones at 2.0 litres per second.

See also Abbot of St Albans, ballcock, flushing, siphonic action.

Clochemerle

Clochemerle by Gabriel Chevallier is the classic comic novel of provincial *France, set in the 1920s. The mayor of the sleepy little town of Clochemerle-en-Beaujolais, to show how progressive the town was, erected a public urinal just opposite the church. All hell broke loose until finally the loo was dynamited. This is the prime example of French lavatorial humour—love it or hate it!

Close stools

Before water-closets became common, lavatories for most people in Britain were either privies or close stools. The close stool was a box with a hole in the top and, inside, a removable container—perhaps a bucket or a pewter *chamber-pot. There was generally a lid, which disguised the object and slightly reduced the smell.

Close stools were kept in bedrooms and in dining rooms. Some were simple; others were elaborate. Henry VIII had a sumptuous one; *see* royalty. Even Queen Victoria used one for much of her long life.

The French called their close stools *chaises percées*, or 'holey chairs', but they had a range of euphemisms too: *chaises d'affaires*, *chaises pertuisées*, *chaises nécessaires*, and so on. Louis XIV had 264 at Versailles, many of

Close stool disguised
as a pile of books

them elegantly upholstered and decorated. Ambassador
Lord Portland was honoured to be received by Louis
on his close stool, and indeed from this throne Louis
announced his engagement to Mme de Maintenon.

Commode
A commode is a bedside table with a cupboard containing
a *chamber-pot, or a chamber-pot concealed in a chair
with a hinged cover; *see* close stool.

Composting lavatories
When human beings—and other animals—excrete on
the ground, the urine sinks in, and the faeces slowly
decompose, enriching the earth in the process. (Note
that both excrement and earth are called 'soil'.) *See*
pigs.

When families settled down and wanted to excrete
repeatedly in the same place, they often created *earth-

closets. Composting lavatories are basically technological developments of earth-closets. They have the same goal—to reduce human waste to a safe fertilizer—and they use similar techniques in more formal ways.

Saving fertilizer and water

The advantages claimed over water-closets is that composting toilets retain the human waste for recycling, rather than throwing it all away (*see* bioloos, eco-loos), and they need no water, which means they can be used even if there is no mains water. This makes them ideal for remote holiday homes, campsites, caravan sites, and other such isolated locations. Furthermore they require little maintenance; some sawdust or shavings have to be added above, and some compost occasionally removed from the bottom. Aerobic decomposition turns most of the excrement into carbon dioxide and water; this results in a 95% reduction in volume; so there is not much compost left in the end.

The chamber is usually primed with a 20cm-deep layer of normal compost and 20cm of wood-shavings, sawdust, or similar organic material to act as 'soak'. Urine filters through, and liquid either collects at the bottom, or runs through into a separate tank or outside, depending on the design. Faeces mix with soak, and gradually decompose. Decomposition is faster if the mixture is agitated and aerated; some such lavatories have stirring mechanisms.

The remarkable result of the decomposition is a moist crumbly compost that is excellent fertilizer and entirely safe; tests in America have shown fewer than 40 coliform bacteria per gram, compared with the National Sanitation Foundation Standard of 200 per gram, and the average for the sludge in a septic tank of 100,000 per gram.

Clivus Multrum

The best-known commercially-available composting loo is the Clivus Multrum, invented in Sweden for summer houses built on ground so rocky that septic tanks aren't diggable. There are several models available, catering for various conditions, from 20 to 120 uses per day. They aim to be complete and self-contained, and to require very low maintenance. You can buy one off the shelf and get it installed in your barn or garden within a few days. The normal Clivus chamber is made of fibreglass, and its floor slopes down towards the access hatch, so that the contents are always moving slowly downhill, which helps aeration.

The Clivus Multrum incorporates a small fan, powered by a battery or a solar panel. This pulls air down through the seat and up the vent pipe, to eliminate smells and assist aeration. Early versions without fans were smelly and liable to attract flies; the manufacturers claim the fan has solved those problems.

The contents need to be emptied only rarely, perhaps once in two or three years, depending on how much it is used. Decomposition is faster in warm weather, and can be accelerated by adding worms, which cause efficient mixing and aeration.

Farallones privy

A privy designed by the Farallones Institute in California has two chambers, side by side. The growing heap should be inspected and turned about once a month. Every six months everything is transferred to the other chamber. The system is said to work well, and produce excellent compost, but this amount of attention and handling means the user has to be a dedicated enthusiast.

The CAT twin-vault privy

Illustration © Centre for
Alternative Technology. (+) 1654
702400, taken from *Fertile waste:
managing your domestic sewage*
by P. Harper

The CAT

The CAT privy (*above*) was designed in Vietnam and used for many years to improve rural sanitation (*see* Vietnam). The Centre for Alternative Technology recommends building your own. Harper and Thorne's *Fertile waste* (*see* Bibliography) provides complete plans for its construction and installation.

The rocking horse

One amazing Dutch device is designed like a rocking horse. You sit and perform on one end, and every now and then rock the entire device. This mixes and aerates the excrement and the soak to speed up decomposition. Eventually the mixture reaches the other end, and can be shovelled out for immediate use in the garden. The

Illustration © Centre for Alternative Technology. (+) 1654 702400, taken from *Fertile waste: managing your domestic sewage* by P. Harper

whole thing is surprisingly compact, and could fit into a medium-sized bathroom. However, the smell might prove to be a problem, since it is freestanding, and so not provided with ventilation.

See also bioloos, eco-loos, pit latrines.

Confession

There is a curious relationship between confession and excretion. Before, you feel uncomfortable, full, guilty; afterwards, relieved, absolved.

In his book *In praise of the stepmother*, Peruvian novelist Vargas Llosa explains how Don Rigoberto takes great care over the regularity of his bowels. After he has defecated 'there invaded him that intimate rejoicing at a duty fulfilled and a goal attained, that same feeling of spiritual cleanliness that had once upon a time possessed him as a schoolboy at La Recoleta, after he had confessed his sins and done the penance assigned him by the father confessor'.

Constipation

Some people defecate three times a day; some once a day; some every third day; and some less than once a week. Any of these frequencies can be regarded as 'normal'. Some people even go without for months. People who would like to defecate more frequently than they actually do regard themselves as constipated. For a simple medical account, see the book *Understanding your bowels* by Dr Ken Heaton.

Constipation seems to have been a common problem in the past, perhaps because the food was often stodgy and without vegetables and other sources of fibre. Henry VIII needed an enema and laxatives (*see* royalty); Martin *Luther and Napoleon were famously constipated.

Constipation is still prevalent in Europe and North America, where hundreds of millions of pounds and dollars are spent on laxatives to bring relief.

Napoleon sat on his 'pot de chambre'

Women and constipation

Family doctors say men rarely complain of constipation. The great majority of sufferers are women, for various reasons. In some cases the abdominal muscles are damaged by childbirth, Caesarian sections, hysterectomies, and so on. Also, the varying hormones in the bloodstream can affect the bowels; women often find their stools are softer before their monthly period.

Women drink less than men, and alcohol is a laxative.

The most common time of day to defecate is in the morning, perhaps after breakfast. Many men go to the lavatory deliberately and even ostentatiously, with a newspaper, and shut themselves away for a time. But women are often busy after breakfast, getting ready for work, or actually working, or getting the children off to school. When they feel they want to go, they suppress the urge, and wait until they are less harassed.

The problem is that anyone who keeps suppressing the urge soon gets used to the feeling of having a distended bowel, and the urge becomes weaker and weaker. Eventually it can be ignored for days.

Many women are persuaded by fashion and by sexist advertising that thin is beautiful, and that they are too fat. One consequence is that they may not like to feel full after meals; so they avoid bulky food. Unfortunately the bulky foods are high in fibre, which is what stimulates regular defecation.

Stress

Men may become constipated by stress. In 1991, Lieutenant Commander W. Brian Sweeney and his colleagues of the US Navy issued a questionnaire about bowel function to 500 deployed marines and sailors aboard the USS *Iwo Jima* LPH 2 during Operation Desert Shield. They discovered that while at home fewer than 4% of the servicemen were constipated (defining constipation as having no bowel movement for more than three days); on board ship, 6% were constipated; and in the field 30% were constipated. Their conclusion was that 'Given the possible ill effects of long-term constipation and because of the associated bothersome symptoms of constipation, consideration should be given to evaluating measures to improve bowel function in the field such as ensuring adequate water intake and possibly supplementing meals with fibre.'

Fibre

Dr Ken Heaton provides some simple tips to avoid constipation:

- Eat lots of fibre.
- Have a regular routine in the morning.
- Eat breakfast.
- Make time to go to the lavatory in the morning— obey the call to stool!
- If your loo seat is high, try putting your feet on a box, or a pile of bricks (*see* squatting).

According to Burkitt, eating plenty of fibre prevents constipation and piles, and lowers the risk of bowel cancer, gallstones, varicose veins, and coronary heart disease.

As long ago as 400 BC, Hippocrates, the most famous doctor of all, is said to have recommended white bread as a treatment for diarrhoea. Even today, the simplest way to increase the fibre in your diet is to eat plenty of wholemeal bread.

Convenience
Convenience means suitability: an advantage: a useful thing: a device for promoting domestic ease or comfort; and so comes to mean a lavatory or water-closet, and especially a building containing several for use by the public, which is therefore called a public convenience; *see* public lavatories.

Converted loos
Victorian public lavatories were built to last, and having outlived their use as conveniences, many have been converted for other purposes. In London, the cavernous loo under Shepherds Bush Green became a snooker hall. The Old Conveniences on Goldhawk Road opposite Ravenscourt Park were turned into a nursery and Montessori school.

Putney Bridge Approach gained Crumbs Sandwich Bar, with graffiti outside, but unfortunately no toilets for customers, while La Piccola Pizzeria in King Street W6 has a superloo next door.

One of the most spectacular is the Burlington Tanning Centre underneath Rosebery Avenue; the elaborate cast-iron railings shout TANNING AT YOUR CONVENIENCE and TOODLE-LOO on the way out.

See also listed lavatories, public lavatories.

Crap

The Oxford English Dictionary says that crap means the husk of grain or chaff, a name of some plants—buckwheat and rye-grass—the residue formed from boiling fat, the dregs of beer or ale, money, and so on. There is no mention of either rubbish or shit. The second edition admits, as the seventh meaning, excrement, defecation (coarse slang), with a first use in 1898, and the verb 'to crap' meaning to defecate, in use since 1846.

In the US, 'crapper' means lavatory; one theory is that the word was brought back by American troops serving in Britain during the First World War who were impressed by Thomas Crapper's products. But if the word 'crap' was used to mean defecate as far back as 1846, Thomas Crapper cannot have been responsible, since he was only ten years old at the time.

Crapper, Thomas

Thomas Crapper was a successful London plumber who was employed by the royal family when they refurbished Sandringham House in the 1880s. He may also have invented the siphonic flush—but that is most unlikely. He certainly did not invent the water-closet.

Crapper was born in 1836—the year before Victoria came to the throne—in the little town of Thorne, near Doncaster in Yorkshire. Thorne was then a thriving port; barges came up the River Don and unloaded cargo on the docks. Thomas's dad was a sailor, and his brothers were dockers, but he must have been unhappy at home, for at the age of eleven, according to Reyburn, he walked 165 miles to London and got himself apprenticed to a plumber in Chelsea. By 1861 he had his own business, which became Thos Crapper & Co, Marlborough Works, Chelsea, and survived until 1966. Thomas lived for the last 13 years of his life at 12 Thornsett Road, Bromley, died on 27 January 1910, and was buried in Elmers End cemetery, near to cricketer W.G. Grace.

Manhole covers

Crapper manhole covers can be found all over the south of England; there are several in Westminster Abbey (one in the cloisters near the deanery is popular for brass-rubbings) and many in the flower-beds both at Sandringham and at Park House next door.

The siphonic flush

The big question is did he really invent the siphonic flush? In one of his advertisements he included a picture of a cistern with the label

Crapper's Valveless Water Waste Preventer
(Patent No. 4,990)
One moveable part only

Wallace Reyburn, Crapper's biographer, is noticeably silent about the date of this patent. Fortunately it is possible at the old patent office to look up all the patents taken out by a particular person. Mr Crapper took out exactly nine plumbing patents, starting with one in 1881 (No. 1628) for ventilating house drains, and ending in 1896 with one (No. 4333) for an improved pipe-joint. None of his patents was No. 4990. None of his patents was for a valveless water-waste preventer (WWP).

During the 1880s various types of siphonic systems were being patented at the rate of about 20 a year—but none by Thomas Crapper.

George Crapper of Marlborough Works—Thomas's nephew—took out in 1897 a patent (No. 724) for 'improvements in or relating to automatic syphon flushing tanks'. But this was more than 40 years after the first siphons.

In fact the first patent for a siphonic flush was taken out by Joseph Adamson in 1853, eight years before Crapper started his business, and 28 years before he took out his first patent.

So alas it seems almost certain that Thomas Crapper did not invent the siphonic flush; he certainly did not patent it, as he implied in his advertising.

See also crap, flushing, water-closets.

Cumming, Alexander

In 1775 Alexander Cumming, mathematician, mechanic, and watchmaker, took out the first British patent for a water-closet.

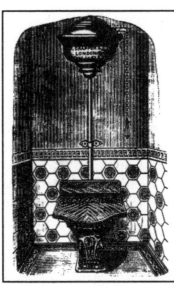

CRAPPER'S

Improved

Registered Ornamental

Flush-down W.C.

With New Design Cast-iron Syphon Water
Waste Preventer.

No 518.

Improved Ornamental Flush-down W.C. Basin
(Registered No. 145,823), Polished Mahogany Seat with flap, New Pattern 3-gallon
Cast-iron Syphon Cistern (Rd. No. 149,284),
Brass Flushing Pipe and Clips, and Pendant
Pull, complete as shown £6 15 0

Born in Edinburgh in 1733, Cumming moved to London and became an accomplished watchmaker in Bond Street. He wrote books about clock and watch work, about the effect on roads of carriage wheels with rims of various shapes, and on the influence of gravity. He became a magistrate and a Fellow of the Royal Society.

His water-closet had a pan with a sliding valve across the bottom. When the user arrived, it contained a few inches of water, held in by this valve. Having finished, the user pulled a lever to slide the valve open and release the contents of the pan to the trap below, and thence into the sewer. The same pull turned on the water to clean the pan, and the valve was then shut so that the pan contained some water for the next person.

His diagram shows the familiar s-bend below the pan, but he didn't invent it; *see* s-bend, Bramah.

D

Dangers to health

Some Victorians worried deeply about health dangers from incompetent sanitation. One man who did something about it was T. Pridgin Teale MA, Surgeon to the General Infirmary at Leeds, who in 1879 published a book entitled *Dangers to health: a pictorial guide to domestic sanitary defects*. This provided cartoon illustrations to show good and bad sanitary practice (*see opposite*).

Plate 1—a house with every sanitary arrangement faulty—was intended to show at a glance the most common sanitary faults of ordinary houses:

A.   Water-closet in the centre of the house.

B.   House drain under floor of a room.

C.   Waste-pipe of lavatory, untapped and passing into soil-pipe of w.c. thus allowing a direct channel for sewer gas to be drawn by the fires LL into the house.

D & E.   Over-flow and waste pipes of bath untapped and passing into soil-pipe ...

H.   Water-closet cistern with over-flow into soil-pipe of w.c. thus ventilating the drain into the roof, polluting the air of the house, and polluting the water of the cistern, which also forms the water supply of the house for drinking and washing ...

This book gets increasingly pungent; Plate 30 is captioned 'How people drink sewage'!

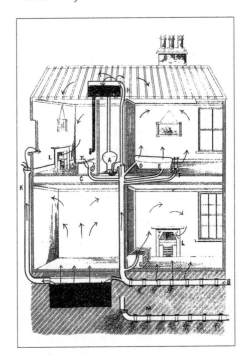

Death

At a banquet given by the Emperor Ferdinand in 1184 in the Great Hall at Erfurt, the floor gave way, precipitating eight princes and many knights and nobles to a sticky end in the cesspit below. One of them was Henry Earl of Schwartzenburg, who had often said of a challenge 'If I do it not, I wish I may sink in a privy!' *See also* royalty.

Judy Garland, Elvis Presley, and Evelyn Waugh all died sitting on their loos.

In 1995 a man was killed in Ryde, on the Isle of Wight, when he sat on a metal lavatory seat which had become live because of a faulty electrical cable.

Many tramps are said to die during the night in the subways of New York because they wake up wanting to relieve themselves, wander over to the edge of the platform, and unthinkingly pee on the live rail. Urine is a solution of salts in water; so it's a good conductor of electricity.

A 1989 survey of 1,230 sudden deaths in Osaka, Japan, revealed that in 8% of the cases the fatal symptoms began in the lavatory; this makes it a less dangerous place than bed (31%) or the bath (17%).

See also Bible, chamber-pots, Essex, royalty.

Desert lavatories

Oil prospectors in the deserts of the Middle East and Australia have left on the landscape their own permanent monuments in tasteful porcelain.

A single prospector just goes over the dunes with his 'dunny-roll' (in Australia) and perhaps scrapes a hole with a heel. When a team is gathered in one place they build a lavatory hut. First cut out one end of a 45-gallon oil drum and punch a few drain holes in the other end. Dig a hole and bury it so that the cut-out end is level with the ground. Across the top, put a platform of marine plywood, or metal if available, with a nine-inch hole in it. Place a normal porcelain lavatory with its outlet pipe down the hole into the drum, and set the loo in concrete. Then put a corrugated-iron or similar hut around it to make a privy.

The lavatory is used as usual, and flushed either with a bucket of water from a separate water butt outside (often another 45-gallon oil drum), or from a makeshift overhead cistern. Lime may be added to the water. The water trap in the s-bend keeps the smell and the insects more or less at bay.

When the prospectors move on they often take the hut with them, and within a few years the wind and the blowing sand erase all other traces of human occupation, except for the porcelain lavatory, immune to erosion, standing proud in the desert sand.

Disabled people

People who are disabled, especially those in wheelchairs, need lavatories with no steps outside, wide doors, enough space inside to turn round, and hand-rails to help mobility. These are called 'accessible' toilets.

Many local authorities in Britain provide accessible public lavatories. Because of frequent damage by vandals, such toilets are often locked, but RADAR provides a solution. RADAR, the Royal Association for Disability and Rehabilitation, has produced a guide to 4,250 public lavatories accessible to disabled people. These are fitted with National Key Scheme locks. Any one of these locks can be opened with an NKS key, and NKS keys can be obtained from local authorities or from RADAR (12 City Forum, 250 City Road, London EC1V 8AF).

See also superloos.

Disease

The greatest advance in human health has come as a direct result of keeping excrement out of the drinking water. Control of malaria by DDT and of bacterial infections by penicillin have had nothing like the same impact as separating the sewage from the fresh water supply.

In the 1830s the death-rate among children under five in England was 24% in the country and 48% in town. In other words, only half the children in towns lived to be five years old. They died from typhoid, paratyphoid, cholera, diarrhoea, dysentery, and gastro-enteritis. Queen Victoria's consort, Prince Albert, died of typhoid in 1861.

In 1985 child mortality was about 1% in the UK, but still frighteningly high in countries without proper sanitation; 20% in Bangladesh, 19% in Haiti, 21% in Nepal, 31% in Sierra Leone.

The leading weapon in the successful fight against disease has been the lavatory, for effective lavatories are the first stage in separating sewage from what we eat and drink. Wash your hands after going, and you are well on your way to avoiding disease. *See also* hygiene.

Dog loos

Dogs are not usually good at defecating in one particular place, as is obvious from paths and pavements used by dog-owners. Nor are they good at reading signs telling them not to foul the pavement.

Armitage Bros of Nottingham make a 'dog loo' which is like a perforated bucket you can bury in your garden, surrounded by stones for drainage. 'Scoop the dog waste into the dog loo, ... flush ... every two weeks (for an average size dog) and add one measure of

the chemical provided.' They supply a free scoop, and helpful instructions on how to 'Train your dog to "Go" before going walkies.'

Duchamp

The celebrated artist Marcel Duchamp (1887-1968) had a curious vision of what was artistic. He sometimes put on show unusual manufactured objects as sculptures; he called them 'ready-mades'. At an exhibition in New York City in 1917 he exhibited a urinal, and called it 'fontaine'. *See also* Sense.

E

Earth-closets

An earth-closet is a lavatory in which dry earth is used to cover excreta. Until Victorian times, the traditional 'place of easement' for people living in the country

Left: earth-sifter; *Right*: earth plug closet

was either a privy with a cesspit, or an earth-closet. Queen Victoria used an earth-closet at Windsor Castle, although many types of water-closet were available. For many years, the earth- and water-closets were rival systems with champions and detractors on both sides.

To make a simple earth-closet, you dug a hole in the ground, leaving the earth piled beside the hole. You could simply squat over the hole, but it was common to build a seat above it. After each visit you shovelled in a little earth on top of the excrement. This process continued until the hole was full, when you covered it over, and dug a new hole a short distance away.

School loo

W. Liddiard patented a commode 'particularly adapted for use indoors', and a multi-seater earth-closet for use in schools (*see opposite*). Any number of units could be bolted together, side by side, and the earth-releasing mechanism

W. Liddiard's Earth-closet for schools

operated from a distance, so that children could be prevented from playing with the device and wasting the earth.

Ash loo
An 1873 dry-ash commode could be filled straight from the fire-grate. The cinders were automatically separated and kept for re-burning, while the fine ash covered the contents of the bucket every time the lid was raised. A later version had a removable drawer instead of a bucket, rather like some *chemical lavatories today.

See also army, bioloos, composting lavatories, eco-loos, Moule.

Eco-loos
Environmentalists disapprove of the use of mahogany and other hardwoods for seats, and of the vast quantities of toilet paper we use; *see* paper. The most serious problem is probably caused by flushing. Each person

in the UK uses about 50 gallons (250 litres) of water every day. Some of this is for washing, but nearly half goes straight down the lavatory. The average lavatory in Britain uses more than two gallons for every flush. New cisterns deliver seven litres, but old ones were bigger, and many of them are still working.

It is absurd to throw away two gallons of this expensive drinkable water every time anyone excretes a teacupful of urine. Not only is the water used—taken from the reservoir and thrown away—but it is also polluted; so it then needs another expensive process of re-purifying in the sewage works.

See bioloos and composting lavatories which provide, in theory, environmentally friendly methods for disposing of human excrement.

See also China, earth-closets, Moule, pit latrines, Vietnam.

Enderby

Anthony Burgess (1917-93) wrote four very funny novels about a poet called Enderby who retires to the lavatory to write his verse.

In the prefatory note to the last of these, *Enderby's dark lady*, Burgess describes how he first thought of the character of Enderby when he was a colonial civil servant in the Sultanate of Brunei. While running a fever, he opened the door to his bathroom and found a man seated in state, apparently writing poetry. This peculiar sight gave him the first promptings for his new hero.

Essex, Earl of

In 1684 Laurence Braddon and Hugh Speke were tried before Judge Jeffreys for alleging that the Earl of Essex had not committed suicide. Part of the evidence reads:

> There was a Closet there, in which was a Close Stool, and that I found shut, and thinking my Lord was there, I would not disturb my Lord, but came down again and stayed a little while, in so much as I thought my Lord by that time might have been come out. I went up again and found no body in the Chamber, but the Closet Door shut still, I went against the Door, and knocked three times and said, My Lord, My Lord, and no body answered: Then I looked through the chink of the Door, between the Door and the Wall, and I could see Blood, and a little part of the Razour.

This story is remarkably similar to that in Judges 3:24; *see* Bible.

Euphemisms

A euphemism is a less distasteful word or phrase used as a substitute for something more offensive. Somehow the object and place in which people excrete has always been thought of as offensive, and we have no simple direct words for them. Both lavatory and toilet originally meant somewhere to wash; a water-closet is a cupboard or small room with a water supply.

A billiard-room lavatory or door-action urinal, water-closet and lavatory

Using such euphemisms seems to be general human behaviour; similar expressions crop up in many cultures and languages; *see* astronauts, Australia, Bible, France, Germany, New Zealand, trains, United States.

Euphemisms for lavatory

Here are some of the words and phrases used in Britain to mean what I call a lavatory: bog, cloakroom, close stool, closet, commode, convenience, garderobe, gents, heads, fakes, khazi, ladies, latrine, lavatory, loo, necessary, petty, place of easement, powder room, privy, shithouse, smallest room, thunder-box, toilet, water-closet, and WC.

Hamilton Ellis suggests that railway companies were responsible for the use of the word toilet. Eighty years ago some railway carriages had a room in which to wash, labelled 'Toilet', opposite one with a water-closet, labelled 'WC'. When the two rooms were combined, the 'Toilet' label was used.

In the sanitary-ware business a 'lavatory' means a wash-basin; a receptacle for excretion is called a 'closet'.

For the verb 'go to the lavatory' we use these euphemisms: explore the geography of the house, go to

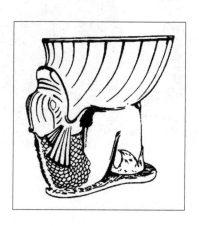

Michael and Phyl's privy—St Michael's

the bathroom/cloakroom/loo/toilet, pay a visit, powder my nose, visit the smallest room, or wash my hands. At school we used to put up a hand, and say 'Please may I be excused?' So 'to be excused' also meant to go to the lavatory.

Euphemisms for faeces (and defecate)
Big jobs, *crap (crap, have a crap, take a crap), dump (do a dump), heap (do a heap), number two, plock (do a plock), plop-plop or plop, poo or pooh, shit, or stool (go to stool).

Euphemisms for urinate
Jimmy Riddle, micturate, pee, piddle, piss, pump ship, slash, strain the potatoes, water the garden/tulips/tomatoes, wee, or widdle and, for men, point Percy at the porcelain, or shake hands with an old friend.

When asked to give a word of advice to newly-commissioned officers, the Duke of Wellington is supposed to have said 'Never neglect an opportunity to pump ship!'

F

Films
Lavatories are rarely seen on television, but films seem positively to revel in excretion. The fashion may have been started by Alfred Hitchcock, who was enthusiastic about lavatories, put one shockingly into *Psycho* (which caused more of a stir at the time than the shower scene),

and once said the length of a film should be in inverse proportion to the endurance of the human bladder.

Arachnophobia has a creepy and thrilling shower-and-lavatory scene.

The opening of *Billy Liar* finds Tom Courtenay in the lavatory.

Kim Basinger appears in the lavatory in the film *Blind Date*.

In *Le Bonheur est dans le Pré*, Michel Serrault's troubles begin with a strike at his place of work—a toilet factory in Paris.

Part of *Carry On at Your Convenience* is set in a sanitary-ware factory.

During *The Conversation*, Gene Hackman imagines a lavatory bubbling over with bloody gore.

In the science-fiction story *Demolition Man*, Sylvester Stallone is transported to a politically correct future, in which there is a penalty for swearing; a box on the wall delivers a ticket and announces 'You are fined one credit for violation of the verbal morality statutes.' He discovers also there is no lavatory paper—people use three sea shells instead—and he is laughed at because he doesn't know how to use the shells. In a scene of rare humour he stands beside one of the boxes and swears again and again, grabs the wad of tickets, and strides off for the loo, saying 'So much for the sea shells!'

Buddies Jim Carrey and Jeff Daniels share three gross lavatorial scenes in *Dumb and Dumber*. First Jeff is driving at high speed along the highway in a ridiculous truck when Jim in the passenger seat gets desperate to pee; so he relieves himself noisily into several empty beer bottles. As he finishes they are stopped by a policeman, who sees the bottles, accuses them of drinking, and starts to drink one himself ... Next comes a crisp scene of sex and violence in the lavatory of a gas station, where Jeff, whose trousers are on fire, inadvertently saves Jim from a dreadful fate. Finally, Jim gives Jeff a giant dose of 'Turbo-lax' to ruin his chances with the girl; Jeff calls at her apartment, nips into the bathroom, and loudly yields to the pressure, only to discover that the lavatory will not flush …

In *Fun with Dick and Jane*, Jane Fonda plots on the loo.

When Michael (Al Pacino) first agrees to join in the violence in *The Godfather*, he arranges a meeting in a restaurant, and then goes to the lavatory and collects a planted gun with which to commit mayhem.

In the opening scenes of *The Italian Job*, master-criminal Noel Coward goes comfortably into the lavatory in prison, with slippers and newspaper.

In *Jurassic Park* a Tyrannosaurus Rex destroys a portaloo and eats the occupant.

During *Lethal Weapon 2* Danny Glover is sitting on the lavatory when he finds out from a note on the toilet roll that it has been rigged to explode when he stands up. There follows a long, hilarious scene in which a vast bomb squad come and work all round him. The denouement is explosive but not lethal.

Mrs Doubtfire features Robin Williams as a father so desperate to see his children he disguises himself and gets a job as a nanny with his estranged wife (Sally Field). In several sequences he goes into a public lavatory as a man and sneaks out as a woman—or the other way round. In one hilarious scene he gets stuck in a restaurant having to go repeatedly into the loo to change sex and costume, each time becoming a little less convincing.

My Favourite Year features Peter O'Toole as a womanizer, who goes into the ladies in a television studio. An old woman says primly 'This is for ladies only!' He replies 'So is this, madam, but every now and then I have to run water through it!'

Tom Cruise goes into the ladies during *Top Gun*, in pursuit of Kelly McGillis, whom he has just met in the bar.

Patsy Kensit gives an extended monologue from the loo in *21*.

In 2001, A Space Odyssey, there is a wonderful moment of lavatorial thought; *see* zero-gravity toilet.

In *Villain*, Richard Burton beats his victim to death in the lavatory.

The Way We Were has Robert Redford being violently sick into Barbara Streisand's lavatory and then apparently making love to her immediately afterwards, without her minding his breath!

In one of *Trainspotting*'s most spectacular special-effects scenes, junkie Renton (Ewan McGregor) plunges head-first into 'the worst toilet in Scotland' and swims down in search of suppositories.

Working Girl has a wedding party in which Harrison Ford marches into the pink chintzy ladies to remonstrate with the heroine Tess (Melanie Griffith)—and in the opening scene Tess as a slaving secretary goes into the men's room to deliver an urgent message to her boss, who humiliates her by demanding that she bring him a roll of loo paper because there isn't any in his stall.

And I am sure there are many more!

Flushing

Flushing—to remove excrement and clean the lavatory—was invented at least 4,000 years ago, and well used by the *Romans. However, our modern systems, and cisterns, were first dreamed up about the end of the eighteenth century.

Early automatics

In 1792, for example, John Ashley patented a device with wires and levers and a heavy valve, which flushed when you stood up, and at the same time opened the valve below the pan. In 1793 Mr Binns of Marylebone patented an automatic water-closet with a 'measurer' that filled with water when you sat down and flushed when you stood up.

A clever version of this was sold by the J.L. Mott Iron Works of New York, in a copper-lined wood cistern. 'When seat is depressed, water passes from the left-hand compartment to the right until it is level in both; when seat is relieved, the water in the right-hand compartment descends and flushes the closet.' An even more advanced version provided a preliminary wash too.

The first patent for a flush using a siphon appears to have been taken out by Joseph Adamson of Leeds in 1853 (No. 904). This was for an automatic flushing

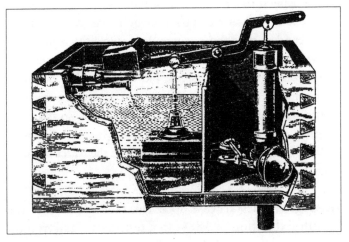

No 11½ Fore-and-after-wash Waste preventing copper-lined Wood Cistern

apparatus with a pivoted cistern, balanced with a counterweight so that when it was as full as required, the weight of water tipped it over, and the contents siphoned out to flush the lavatory, urinal, or sewer.

This arrangement is reminiscent of the *slop-closet, but the idea of the siphon seems to have been new with Adamson; Thomas *Crapper surely didn't invent it, since in 1853 he was only seventeen years old and an apprentice in London.

George Jennings

In 1854 George Jennings, having perhaps seen the potential of Adamson's idea, took out patent No. 1017, which describes beautifully the principle of the siphon. He had:

> a cistern, which is supplied from a water main or other source, and the supply regulated by a ball-cock or float, as is well understood. From this cistern the longer leg of a syphon descends to the water-closet or otherwise, the shorter leg of the syphon being in the cistern, and the bend of the syphon comes just above the ordinary level of water in the cistern. In order to cause the water to descend from the cistern, the water level is raised, and this, by preference, is done by introducing a plunger into the water, which raises the water level, so that it comes above the bend of the syphon, when the syphon will immediately come into action, and the water in the cistern run off.

Jennings's Pedestal Vase won the Gold Medal at the Health Exhibition of 1884. In a test, a two-gallon flush completely removed 10 apples averaging one-and-a-half inches diameter, one flat sponge about four-and-a-half inches diameter, three air vessels (which were like crumpled pieces of paper), plumber's smudge coated over the pan, and four pieces of paper adhering closely to the soiled surface.

See also Abbot of St Albans, ball-cock, cistern, siphonic action.

France
French words for lavatory include *la latrine*, *la salle dieau*, *les chiottes* (rude), *les sanitaires*, *les toilettes*, and *les WC* (pronounced 'vaysay'), and 'to go to the lavatory' is *aller au fond du couloir* or *faire un petit tour la bas*. Their euphemisms used to be Anglophobic—anglaise was *surtout une sorte de garderobe*, and advertisements used to offer *cabinets à l'Anglaise*.

Louis XIV had a remarkable range of *chaise percées*; *see* close stools.

Frenchmen used to be entirely blasé about peeing in public, and Paris was famous for its many prominent *pissoirs*, in which the users were entirely visible to passers-by in the street, except for a narrow screen at waist height.

One result was that Paris gained a reputation as the pissing centre of the world. A British holiday poster exhorting people to take a ferry from Essex to the European mainland with the slogan HARWICH FOR THE CONTINENT was often given a graffito second line: PARIS FOR THOSE WHO ARE NOT!

Funnels

According to Ms Lore Harp, President of the Aples Corporation in San Mateo, California, 90% of all women do not sit on the toilet seat; they have been taught to squat over it for reasons of hygiene. So she invented 'La funelle', a disposable coated paper funnel with a 12-cm tube, that women can use to wee while standing up.

A rival company, Sani-fem, sells the Freshette—a portable female urinal—by mail order from Downey California, and claims it is great for travellers, campers, hikers, and cross-country athletes, as well as those with knee, back, or muscular problems. The regular Freshette is an 'environmentally sound, palm-sized, feather-light and reusable anatomically designed funnel ...' The regular tube is five-and-a-half inches long, but they can supply longer tubes for use in a wheelchair or in bed. They also sell disposable, biodegradable Freshettes.

G

Germany

In German there are many words for lavatory. The official word is *Toilette*, and this appears on signs (like the English 'Toilets'); WC (again pronounced 'vaysay') appears on the door in the hotel or restaurant. The usual word is *Klo*, which is probably short for *Klosett*, a slightly old-fashioned expression, but still in use. The normal label on the door used to be 00, pronounced nul nul.

Standard army slang is *Donnerbalken* ('thunder-plank'), which is the subject for a rude song. More vulgar is Scheißhaus (shithouse).

The normal expression for 'to go to the too' is *auf's Klo gehen*. Also common are *auf die Toilette gehen*, *für kleine Mädchen* (or *Jungen*) *gehen*, and *mal müssen*; so *ich mal müss* means 'I must go ...' More specific options are *Urin ablassen*, *Stuhlgang machen*, *pissengehen*, *pinkelngehen*, and *scheißengehen*; so, for example, *ich gehe pinkeln* means 'I am going to pee'.

Ghost town

The ghost town of Virginia City in south-western Montana, not far from Yellowstone Park, boasts a single hotel, with a balcony in front. At the end of the balcony is a double-decker privy, one seat above the other. The holes are off-set; but if you choose to 'sit' on the ground floor, remember not to lean to the right!

God and Goddess

According to Sir John *Harington, the Roman god of the lavatory was Stercutius. The goddess assigned for this whole business was Dea Cloacina, whose statue was apparently found in a great Privy or Jakes of Rome.

See also praying in the privy.

Gongfermors

Gongfermors or gong-scourers were men who went round emptying medieval privies and cesspits.

Where there was no convenient moat or stream, people dug a pit, or used a removable barrel. In either case the sewage had to be removed in due course. In 1281, 13 men took five nights to clear the *cloaca* at Newgate Prison—on triple pay! At Hampton Court in Henry VIII's time, the gongfermors had a formidable task; *see* history, nightmen.

Graffiti

Some people have a compulsion to write on the walls of public lavatories, probably because they have spare time and a public place to write, but can create the work in private—and it remains anonymous. Unfortunately, most of the things they write on the walls are rude, crude and not very funny.

I have seen a few that amused me; for example in a university biochemistry department GOD IS ALIVE AND WELL AND WORKING ON A LESS AMBITIOUS PROJECT. And along the bottom of a partition between cubicles in the office loo, BEWARE LIMBO DANCERS!

The habit of writing on the walls is far from new. On a loo wall in the city of Herculaneum, buried by ash from the eruption of Vesuvius in AD 79, is written

APOLLONIVS MEDICVS TITI IMP. HIC CACARIT BENE. In other words, 'Apollonius, physician of Emperor Titus, had a good crap here.'

A survey by the London Regional Passengers' Committee in the stations of the London Underground and British Rail found that 77% of men's cubicles were adorned with graffiti, and 79% of women's. An anonymous spokeswoman said 'The answer is simple— we sit there longer, write faster, and have dirtier minds!'

Grimthorpe

Edmund Beckett Denison, first Lord Grimthorpe (the designer of Big Ben), was annoyed by slovenly visitors. He introduced a cunning device into his lavatory; once the user had locked the door it could not be opened until the loo had been flushed.

H

Harington, Sir John

John Harington, born in 1560, is often credited with the invention of the *water-closet, although similar devices had long been in use. Harington's character and behaviour were elegantly described in an essay by Lytton Strachey:

> An old miniature shows a young man's face, whimsically Elizabethan, with tossed-back curly hair, a tip-tilted nose, a tiny point of a beard, and a long single earring, falling in sparkling drops over a ruff of magnificent proportions. Such was John Harington—a courtier, a wit, a scholar, a poet, and a great favourite with the ladies. Suddenly, inspired, he invented the water-closet. Then, seizing his pen, he concocted a pamphlet after the manner of Rabbelais—or, as he preferred to call him, 'the reverent Rabbles'—in which extravagant spirits, intolerable puns, improper stories, and sly satirical digs at eminent personages were blended together into a preposterous rhapsody, followed by an appendix—written, of course, by his servant—could a gentleman be expected to discuss such details?—containing a minute account, with measurements, diagrams, and prices, of the new invention. The metamorphosis of Ajax—for so the book, with a crowningly deplorable pun, was entitled—created some sensation. Queen Elizabeth was amused ... she approved of his invention; and eventually she set the fashion by installing one of them in Richmond Palace, with a copy of the Ajax hanging from the wall.

Harrington's Ajax. He
called it Ajax because
the standard word for a
lavatory was a jakes

History (potted)

There seem to have been lavatories in the neolithic stone
huts of Scara Brae in the Orkney Islands, used perhaps
6,000 years ago. At Mohendro Daro in India, about
2750 BC, there were privies with seats connected to a
drain.

About 4,000 years ago in the Indus Valley, now
Pakistan, many houses had flushing lavatories, and at
about the same time King Minos's magnificent palace at
Knossos in Crete had loos with wooden seats, earthenware
wash-out pans, and reservoirs for flushing water.

Abbey lavvies

Many abbeys in Britain had piped water before AD
1200. Monks were well aware of the dangers of disease,
and built efficient latrines—usually in a wing next to
the dormitory—with many seats, because their strict

timetable meant the monks all had to relieve themselves at the same time. Sometimes, as at Furness, the seats were back to back.

At Fountains Abbey in Yorkshire, there was a latrine block for the choir monks on the east side of the River Skell, and one in the middle of the river, with lavatories on two floors, for the lay brothers. When the abbey was rebuilt in the twelfth century, the engineers changed the course of the river by 26 metres, and constructed a stone-lined drain along its course with a continuous flow from the river to flush both sets of lavatories. Many so-called 'secret passages' in abbeys were in reality drains leading to the main sewer.

See also Abbot of St Albans.

Royal loos and flush

Royal residences provide some information about lavatories, but alas succeeding generations tend to replace them when better ones are available.

At Hampton Court, Henry VIII's courtiers used a large communal lavatory designed on the garderobe principle, called the Great House of Easement (*see below*). There were two rows set back to back on each of two floors, with views over the east and west fronts of the palace. Each seat was a single plank of oak with holes at regular two-foot intervals; so at breaks in court proceedings the loos must have been quite cosy.

The effluent went down angled chutes into a communal brick drain, which ran under the moat and into the River Thames. However, there was no flushing system; so after the court had been in residence for a month, the smell from below must have been ripe, and the King's gong-scourers would be faced with head-high chambers full of waste to clear out.

Kristina Ferris and Mike Scorer © *The Independent*

Henry VIII himself preferred to use a close stool; *see* royalty. For an Elizabethan interlude, *see* Harington.

Seventeenth century

In the 1660s, Samuel Pepys recorded in his diary that he had 'a very fine close stool' in his drawing room, and a cesspit in his cellar. He also writes of taking a lady to the theatre in 1663. She wanted to go to the loo, but there was none in the theatre 'so I was forced to go out of the house with her to Lincoln's Inn walks, and there in a corner she did her business, and was by and by well, and so into the house again ...'

During the early 1690s, at least 10 water-closets were built at the great mansion of Chatsworth, with cedar-wood, brass fittings, and bowls of alabaster—or marble for the duke and duchess. The water came from the hills above the house.

Ordinary people living in the country generally had a *privy, which was just a hole in the ground with seats above. In the growing cities, people used privies where they had the room, even if it meant digging pits in their own cellars. But many people simply used *chamber-pots, and emptied the contents into the street outside. When they tipped from an upstairs window they traditionally called a warning of 'Gardy loo!' which was probably a corruption of the French *regardez l'eau*, meaning 'watch out for the water!' (*see below*).

Trevelyan writes of the early morning in Edinburgh about 1700:

> Far overhead the windows opened, five, six, or ten storeys in the air, and the close stools of Edinburgh discharged the collected filth of the last 24 hours into the street. It was good manners for those above to cry 'Gardy-loo!' before throwing ... early in the morning it was perfunctorily cleared away by the City Guard. Only on a Sabbath morn it might not be touched, but lay there all day long, filling Scotland's capital with the savour of a mistaken piety.

Furthermore, in the absence of public lavatories, men walked the streets carrying buckets and huge cloaks, offering for a 'bawbee' (half a penny) the services of the cloak and bucket to anyone desperate to relieve themselves.

Nineteenth century

By about 1830, the population of London had risen to two million. The raw sewage seeped through inadequate drains into the River Thames, which was made even fouler by waste from slaughterhouses and tanneries. As a result of this tide of filth, the middle of the nineteenth century saw a dreadful outbreak of cholera in Britain; in 1849, more than 55,000 people died of it.

Such campaigners as John Snow and Florence Nightingale pointed out the link between disease and lack of hygiene. Gradually demand grew for a continuous supply of clean piped water, and for proper *sewers. In the dry summer of 1858 the smell of drifting excrement on the banks of the

Thames became so intolerable that the Great Stink was debated in parliament, where the curtains were soaked in chloride of lime to enable the members to breathe.

So Victorian engineers began to build proper sewers, and as piped water became available, demand grew for hygienic loos. Between 1860 and 1880 there was a flood of new *water-closets.

Hopper closet

The hopper closet was a simple lavatory that may well have been in use for hundreds of years. It could be cheaply made of earthenware in two parts, and was perhaps one of the first aspirations of poor Victorian working-class people.

The flush was hopeless. A thin stream of water came in through one hole in the front, and spiralled weakly down to the bottom, only rarely disturbing any of the stuff sticking to the sloping walls. As a result, hopper closets were much more disgusting than basic privies with wooden seats, but nevertheless they were better than nothing for those with no access to a hole in the ground, and they were advertised

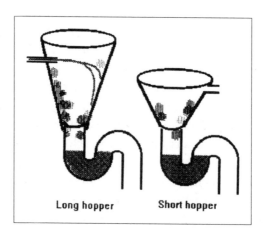

Long hopper   Short hopper

as suitable for prisons, mills, etc. Hoppers were still being manufactured in Britain in 1910.

Hellyer's jar

Hellyer's jar closet was similar to a hopper, although it had a rim 'rounded and of sufficient width to allow use by any person in a sitting position without the use of a wooden seat'. The luxury extras of 'haunch pieces' of teak or vulcanite were available for those who found the rim too narrow.

How to make a loo

A few lavatories are made from stainless steel or aluminium (*see* Royal Navy, superloos), and some from fireclay, but most are made from *vitreous china. Liquid clay slip is pumped along pipes and tubes into the bottom of plaster moulds, hung in rows in the factory. The moulds fill, and a little extra runs up into a polythene tube. The water is slowly absorbed by the plaster of Paris, and within an hour and a half the moulds can be removed to leave finger-hard closets.

These are fettled—wiped with a sponge—and spray glazed either by hand or electrostatically by machines, with a robot arm to spray inside the bowl.

They then go into the kiln, of which the largest are gas-fired tunnel kilns, 50 metres long. A 'car', loaded with perhaps 30 pieces, takes 13 hours to go through, reaching its maximum temperature of 1,200° C for about three hours in the middle. Each closet shrinks by 12½% in the kiln.

Loo makers

Sanitary-ware manufacture has a long and complex history. For example, in 1817 a small pottery with a

bottle-neck kiln was built beside the Trent and Mersey canal in the village of Armitage, near Rugeley in Staffordshire. The pottery changed hands many times, and in 1867 was bought at auction by the Rev'd Edward Johns. It traded as Edward Johns until 1960; *see* United States.

Meanwhile, in 1851, John Shanks set up as a plumber in Paisley, Scotland, and within 10 years began to make water-closets and patent improvements. The Shanks family firm prospered for 120 years. In 1969 the two companies merged to form Armitage Shanks, in whose main factory at Armitage about 8,000 closets are now made every working day.

Hygiene

Urine is normally sterile, but faeces contain dangerous bacteria and other pathogens—things that can cause disease—so it's important to wash your hands after defecating. Washing does not make them sterile, but should remove the worst of the contamination, and prevent passing it on to others.

Toilet seats

Can you catch diseases from lavatory seats? Research in America and in Germany has shown that colonies of many species of bacteria can be found on seats, especially on the rim. Such bacteria are almost harmless on your skin; before they can invade they need to get to a soft entry point, such as the mouth or nose. Therefore you are not likely to catch disease from a lavatory seat, as long as you wash your hands. Contaminated toilet paper probably has greater potential as a direct source, partly because bacteria can survive on it better than on hard seats.

However, people have been known to catch hepatitis and dysentery from toilet seats; also fungal infections. An outbreak of puerperal fever due to streptococcal infection in Chelmsford in 1987 was thought to have been spread in part by toilet seats or a shower. A recurrent outbreak of viral gastro-enteritis on board ship in 1989 seemed to be spread between people using shared toilet facilities.

Americans have always been concerned about the transmission of disease via public lavatory seats, and often provide 'hygienic paper covers' in wall dispensers—sometimes known as butt gaskets—so the sitter can avoid touching the seat.

However, public lavatories do present some dangers, even when clean and well maintained. The flushing process generates an aerosol which carries bacteria (*see* aerosols) and 1994 research sponsored by the Association of Makers of Soft Tissue Papers showed that hot-air hand driers actually broadcast bacteria; cotton towels and especially paper towels are much safer.

I

Igloos

People who live in the far north of Canada and the United States used to be nomadic; their waste was eaten by their dogs or simply left behind. Now they live in fixed towns, and sewage disposal has become a problem because the ground is permafrost; even in summer it remains frozen solid just below the surface; so digging holes is impossible, and water cannot be carried in underground pipes.

People on the edge of town use honey-buckets—plastic bags in bins, which are collected from outside the houses and dumped in a landfill site. Citizens of Inuvik (population 3,200) use the Utilidor system; a large tube a metre or so off the ground runs for 7.5km round the centre of town, carrying within it separate pipes for hot water, cold water, and sewage. The hot water, direct from the power station, supplies district heating, and protects the other two pipes from frost. The sewage is then delivered to a three-cell lagoon treatment facility.

See also bottom of the world.

India

I have watched men squatting communally in the fields in India, but in most of the country excrement is not used systematically to enrich the soil, as it is in *China.

People in rural areas often use pour-flush latrines with a pan and water-seal trap, which may be either directly above the pit or a few metres away. Since most people use water for anal cleaning, they need water in the latrine anyway. Two or three litres is enough for a

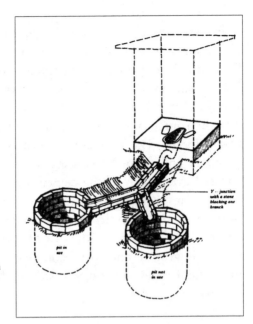

Kjell Torstensson. From *Sanitation without water* by Uno Winblad and Wen Kilama (Macmillan, 1985)

flush, and the water trap keeps smells and flies out of the latrine.

After a year or two the pit has to be emptied. Removing fresh sewage is unpleasant and dangerous to health. In the two-pit design, one pit is used until it is full; then the flow is switched to the other pit. The contents of the first can be left for another year to decompose, after which the compost is far less offensive.

See also composting lavatories, earth-closets, pit latrines, Vietnam.

Inspiration
Bob Olley has lived all his life in South Shields, where lavatories are called 'netties', which according to local legend stems from the Roman occupation, since the Italian word for a row of toilets is *gabinetti*. For 17

years Bob was a miner, but the pit closed, and he set out to make a living as an artist; you'll find him in the Gambling Man Gallery in Wapping Street.

Bob was born within the smell of the Westoe Netty, a public urinal under a railway bridge, and says it was the source of his inspiration, as well as one of his first subjects. The men coming out of the pubs filled the netty and formed a waiting queue outside. Graffiti covered every inch of the cement-rendered walls, and the ancient flush never succeeded in clearing the trough of fag ends and tram tickets. His painting of the Westoe Netty, which is now closed, is a wonderful kaleidoscope of colour, graffiti, and social comment, but too rich for these small pages; so here, entitled *The Day Dreamer*, is an early inspiration.

© Bob Olley 1977

Iraqi cubicle

In *Bravo two zero*, his horrific book about *SAS operations in the Gulf War, Andy McNab describes how, after capture, he was led to a big room with a row of a dozen doors, close together. The guard pushed him inside one, shut the door, and fastened bolt and padlock.

The darkness was absolute. There was a gagging stench of faeces. Andy got down on his hands and knees and felt his way around. He soon discovered, in the middle of the tiny space, two porcelain footpads either side of a hole about eight inches in diameter. No wonder his new bedroom stank.

J

Jakes

Jakes was the normal word for lavatory or privy from the sixteenth century to the eighteenth. In *King Lear* II, ii, 74–6 Shakespeare wrote 'I will tread this unbolted villain into mortar, and daub the wall of the jakes with him.' The origin is obscure, but may be from Jaques' or Jack's house. *See also* Harington.

Japan

'Japanese-style' lavatories, designed for squatting rather than sitting, look rather like bidets sunk into the floor, and have been called 'bombsites' by occidental travellers. However, the world's most advanced 'western-style' lavatories are also made in Japan.

Ancient loos

The most ancient Japanese lavatory yet found, in Nara Prefecture, was built in the old capital (Fujiwara-kyo) about AD 700. Analysis of the fossilized excrement showed the users ate whole sardines, and 30 different kinds of nuts and fruits. They also suffered from parasitic worms. Apparently these people did not use fire for cooking, and ate only raw food.

By the eighth century there were separate lavatories for men and women in Fukuoka City, according to the cholesterol levels in the fossilized remains.

There was a flush toilet at the Koumyousen Ji Temple near Kyoto in the thirteenth century.

The Kochi loo

What is claimed to be the most environmentally friendly public lavatory was built in 1993 in Kochi Prefecture by the Shimanto River, said to be the cleanest river in Japan. The water is recirculated, and has not been changed after its first year, despite the visits of 10,000 people.

Noises off

Japanese ladies visiting the lavatory in restaurants and other public places, worried about the embarrassing noises they might make, carry with them a little electrical device like a flashlight, which makes the sound of a lavatory flush. This acceptable noise covers any other noises that might occur. Upmarket toilets have wall-mounted versions.

High technology

The most advanced lavatories in the world are made in Japan by Toto. Their simplest model is the Warmlet, which has a heating element in the seat. Toto once advertised this with the slogan 'Your bottom will like it after three tries. Don't let people say behind your back that you have a dirty bottom!'

The Washlet (*below*) is much more complex; it includes a bidet and warm-air drier, with a bank of electronic controls that would not be out of place on the Starship Enterprise. For each function—warm, wash, and dry—there is an on/off button and a dial to control the temperature. Further dials control water and air pressure.

When you press the spray button, a nozzle extends about two inches at 43° below the back of the seat, and sprays you as long as you hold the button down. Then the nozzle retracts again, and the tip is washed clean. Meanwhile you can dry yourself on a breeze of warm air.

The Washlet is immensely popular in Japan; allegedly 720,000 were sold in 1993 at more than £600 each; yet only 720 were sold in the whole of Europe.

For women who cannot live without it, there is now the Petit Washlet, a portable battery-powered bidet which folds and collapses to fit into a handbag.

Jersey

The Territorial Army unit on the Channel Island of Jersey was looking for a useful community exercise in 1992; so at the request of the Customs and Excise Department they built a new water-tank and lavatory alongside the customs hut on the Ecrehous, a chain of rocky islets between the north-east coast of Jersey and France. It was the first flushing lavatory on the Ecrehous, and it raised a mighty stink among those with holiday retreats there. Brigadier Raoul Lempriere-Robin is quoted as saying 'Why can't they make do with an Elsan? ... The toilet is now the grandest structure on the Ecrehous ... To put it bluntly, it has been a bugger's muddle all along.'

Jeyes

During the second half of the eighteenth century, controversy reigned over cleanliness; there were deodorizers to replace unpleasant smells, antiseptics to prevent decay, and disinfectants to kill germs, but which was the most important? John Jeyes made his name by combining all three; in 1877 he patented 'Jeyes Fluid'. He is said to have been so fat that he had to be helped on and off with his boots and pushed upstairs to his office. He died in 1892, leaving only £585 17s and 10d.

However, despite this rather shaky start, Jeyes is now a household name in hygiene and cleaning. The company still does vital research, and in one room in the laboratories at Thetford are no less than 268 computerized lavatories, flushing every few minutes, checking the performance of each product.

Jokes on the jakes

People have been making lavatorial jokes since they had lavatories and a sense of humour.

Sir John *Harington makes dozens of jokes in his book *The metamorphosis of Ajax*. The text opens with a story about M. Jaques Wingfield, being introduced by a maid (too shy to say the word 'jakes') as M. Privie Wingfield—although Harington takes half a page to tell the story.

Often heard on the radio is a story about the theft of the lavatory seat from the police station. The police are looking into it, but they've got nothing to go on ...

When I was at school, and we wanted to say that one of our friends was dim or stupid or mad, we would say he was Harpic, because that brand of lavatory cleaner used the slogan 'Harpic means clean round the bend.'

I am fond of an American limerick:

One day a fellow called Hyde
Fell into a privy and died.
The next day his brother
Fell into another,
And now they're interred side by side.

K

Kangaroos

A baby kangaroo at birth is tiny. Deaf, blind, and bald, it clambers with great difficulty up mum's fur to her pouch, and there it lives, warm, protected, and attached to a nipple, for up to eight months. During this period, all its excrement has to go into the bottom of the (waterproof) pouch.

I had imagined a filling cesspool in there, but in fact mum regularly licks baby and pouch clean, and leaves both wet with saliva. This helps keep the baby warmed by good contact with her skin, until it starts to grow fur at around five months.

Korean monasteries

A former monk and a former nun tell me that lavatories in Korean monasteries are built to a standard pattern.

The men's and women's rooms are essentially the same inside—rows of about five pairs of cubicles, back to back, with a wall down the middle between them. Each cubicle has side walls, but no wall or door in front; you just walk along until you find one unoccupied.

There is no lavatory bowl. The central floor plank is missing; you squat astride the gap; the waste goes through and falls three metres to the ground below, followed by whatever you use to cleanup—water, leaves, or paper—and a handful of ashes or straw.

On the ground below, the composting is simple. A layer of leaves or straw is added every two or three days, and after about three months local farmers come and collect all the compost to spread on their fields. The building is so well ventilated, and the composting so efficient, there is no offensive smell.

The upper part of the outer walls is louvred; so as you squat you can look out through the wall to the lovely countryside beyond. On the wall are mantras to chant at each phase of the process:

Chant for entering the toilet
To eliminate, and to eliminate again, is such a joy! May I eliminate the three poisons (avarice, anger, and foolishness) in this same way, so that I become, in an instant, free from wrongdoing.

> *Ohm halodaya sabaha.* (Three times)

Chant for washing the body
Emptying and becoming clean is the greatest pleasure. It is making a dream become reality. I fervently hope that all in the universe will quickly reach the Pure Land.

> *Ohm hanamalihae sabaha.* (Three times)

Chant for washing the hands
Water puts out even the fiercest of fires. My eyes are on fire, my ears are on fire, my heart is on fire. The clear, cool waters of Buddha's teachings are the only way to put these fires out.

> *Ohm chugalaya sabaha.* (Three times)

Chant for ridding oneself of uncleanliness
Let's wash away suffering just as we wash away this dirt. As our hearts become cleaner, we may become more tranquil. During this life my only wish is to reach that faraway land which has not even a speck of dust.

> *Ohm saliyae bahye sabaha.* (Three times)

L

Latin literature

The *Romans loved their loos, and it is hardly surprising that lavatorial references are common in Latin literature.

Catullus, bitchy poetry critic, suggested that the Annals of Volusius would make better loo-paper than poetry—*Annales Volusi, cacata charta*.

In Catullus's Poem 39, Egnatius constantly smiles, showing unnaturally white teeth. Catullus suggests (lines 18-21) this is because people in Spain have unusual toothpaste:

> *quod quisque minxit, hoc sibi solet mane*
> *dentem atque russam defricare gingivam*
> *ut, quo ista vester expolitior dens est*
> *hoc te amplius bibisse praedicet loti.*

This may be translated as:

> What each person pees, he regularly rubs on his teeth
> and gums in the morning; so the shinier your teeth are,
> the more of your piss you must have drunk!

In Ostia, a wall-painting of the seven sages of Greece shows each with a piece of lavatorial advice in verse. Here is one of them:

> *ut bene cacaret, ventrem palpavit Solon.*
> To crap better, Solon rubbed his tummy.

Lavatory

For at least 500 years a lavatory was a room for washing, a basin, a bath, or a laundry.

After about 1850 (*OED*) lavatory came to mean also a receptacle into which a person can urinate or defecate. In the sanitary-ware business today, a lavatory is a wash-basin; a bowl for excretion is a closet; *see* euphemisms.

Lighting-up loo

Women are apparently irritated by men leaving the seat up; so some bright spark in the USA has invented a loo that lights up in the dark. When the infrared sensor detects a person approaching, the light glows green if the seat is down and red if it is up.

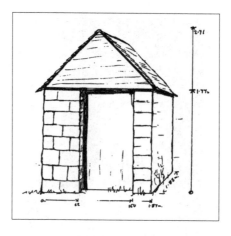

Listed lavatories and recorded privies

Around the country, a number of lavatories, mainly public ones, are listed, which means they may not be demolished or altered. Many others have been recorded by the Royal Commission on Historical Monuments.

At Dalton in North Yorkshire there is an eighteenth-century double privy with a dovecote on top at Old Dunsa Bank Farm, while at Winters Farm, Pulborough in Sussex (*above*) the dressed stone privy has a tiled roof with weather-boarded gable ends.

The Amblehurst Manor privy at Wisborough Green is built of odd-sized bricks with windows; the clay-tiled roof has a lead cap.

There is a listed privy in Hessle Road, Hull, occupying a secluded spot by Pickering Park, and its roof sports an unusual gable ventilator. A three-holer eighteenth-century privy at Townsend House, Leominster has early sash windows and dado panelling, and forms almost a perfect cube.

The Grade II listed gents in Court Road, Balsall Heath is in the middle of a dubious area of Birmingham; but it was built in 1890, and is 'probably the most magnificent toilet we have got' according to Christopher Hargreaves, the Council's Head of Conservation. It has decorated panels of geometric and scrolled grotesque patterns. A listed urinal of similar design stands in Vyse Street, Hockley, in the Jewellery Quarter. There is yet another at the railway bridge at Snow Hill.

On forestry land near Neath in West Glamorgan is a listed loo built 200 years ago in the style of a circular pigsty. At Pratt's Farmhouse at Broadclyst in Devon the thatched privy stands over a stream, like the two-seater with shale walls and a slate roof at Uwchygarreg near Machynlleth. The privies at Little Vachery and Charlton have tiled roofs over a mixture of brick and wood.

There's a lavatory by Inigo Jones at Charlton House in Greenwich, and an elegant one behind the law courts at Star Yard, WC2, but high on my list are the *public lavatories built in 1897 by the London and North-Western Railway at South End Green in Hampstead. Green-and-white-tiled walls, black-and-white-chequered floor, and eight Doulton's urinals, not to mention chamfered panelled doors and screens under decorative circular cast-iron vents.

Finally, the door of a privy in Westerdale, Yorkshire, has a massive stone lintel; what do you make of this curious inscription carved in it:

WHATSOEVER THOU TAKEETH IN
HAND REMEMBER THY END

Locks

The locks on lavatory doors—at least the kind with a rack and pinion that moved a label to say ENGAGED when the lavatory was occupied—were invented by Arthur

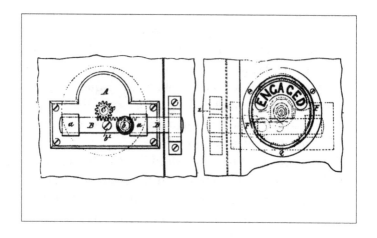

Ashwell. He took out a patent in 1882 (No. 781), and another, for an improved version, in 1885 (No. 6928). The improved mechanism was better designed and easier to fit. Furthermore it not only incorporated a hidden spring 'which renders the action of the bolt smooth and noiseless', but also allowed for notches to be included for locks on board sea-going vessels to 'remove the liability of the bolt to be shot or withdrawn by the rolling of the vessel at sea'.

London
In 1995, according to the *Evening Standard*, Greater London boasted 3,226,909 household lavatories, but 13,816 households had no inside flush toilet.

Long drops
At Stockhorn there is a 2000-foot drop down the Alps, which gives you severe vertigo if you are foolish enough to look down, while beyond Chamonix is a toilet with a direct drop into the snow, so that everything is lovingly preserved. West of Zermatt near the Cabane de Bertol

was a two-seater privy with a drop of a few hundred feet.

About 10 miles north-west of Hexham, in Northumberland National Park, there is a lovely privy built in the early 1800s at the remote Lower Roses Bower farm, reputed locally to have the longest drop in England. The stone hut is perched 40 feet over a sheer drop into the Warks Burn (above).

Most houses in Ladakh in the western Himalayas have a first-floor room with a drop hole in the floor. The family excrete on earth and/or ashes on the floor, and then push the mixture through the hole; it drops into a room like a shed, reached from the outside.

In Bhutan, in the eastern Himalayas, the traditional farmhouse has a latrine built on a first-floor balcony, often with a fall into the pig-pen; *see also* pigs.

My favourite long drop is from the toilet on top of the world, at the Potala Palace in Lhasa, a magnificent white stone building from the front. If you have a chance to look round the back, however, you will see one small room corbelled out at the top, with a hole in the floor,

Kjell Torstensson. From *Sanitation without water* by Uno Winblad and Wen Kilama (Macmillan, 1985)

and below it a brown stain smeared down at least 20 metres of once-white stone wall.

See also Korean monasteries.

Martin Luther

Protestant theologian Martin Luther (1483-1546) was the major protagonist in the German Reformation. He suffered dreadfully from constipation and haemorrhoids, and it has been said that there would not have been a Protestant Reformation if Martin Luther's bowels had been more regular.

According to Wallace, Luther was known to cry out to the devil 'I have shit in the pants, and you can hang them around your neck and wipe your mouth with it.' He boasted he could 'drive away the evil spirit with a single fart'.

M

Macerators

A macerating lavatory is rather like a waste-disposal unit on the kitchen sink; it chews up what is put into the loo so that everything can be pumped away down small-bore pipes—as narrow as 22mm—rather than the 10cm demanded by normal gravity-driven outlets. The outflow can be pumped up to 50 metres horizontally, and even 5 metres upwards.

This means you can put a macerating loo in a concrete cellar, or a corner of the house without any existing large-pipe plumbing, where you could not possibly put a conventional loo. Also some models can dispose of tampons and similar things, without blocking. The disadvantage is that macerators are expensive, and use electricity.

Mecca

Throughout the UK there have been requests from Muslims to reorient their loos. The problem is that to face Mecca while using the lavatory breaches the Islamic code of personal conduct, and many council houses were built a long time ago, when the Asian community was small.

Mirror, mirror

In 1990, the downstairs lavatory of Uri Geller's mansion Sonning Court had all four walls and the ceiling covered with mirrors and gold; so visitors could sit and reflect *ad infinitum*.

Mississippi view

The Minnesota World Trade Center towers 35 floors over downtown St Paul. Apparently, the upper three floors were initially rented out to a rich sheikh, who had the offices tailored to his wishes. The men's toilet is breathtaking; as you sit enthroned, on one side of you is a partition, but on the other side, a glass window the full height and width of the room provides a stunning view of the Mississippi River valley.

Moist toilet tissue

Moist toilet tissue appeared during the 1990s in supermarkets and chemists in Britain. Using it is like washing yourself with a cool, wet, scented flannel, and it leaves you feeling a bit damp—but perhaps it cleans well.

The fluid ingredients of one such product are water, propylene glycol, polysorbate 20, phenoxyethanol, cetrimonium bromide, and seven other compounds, but then it is 'lightly fragranced', and has been 'dermatologically tested', according to the packet, which also says 'The tissue is thick and soft for effective, gentle cleansing. It leaves you feeling really fresh. Use it after dry toilet tissue.' This last instruction is rather surprising, since it leaves you feeling damp enough to think seriously about using dry tissue afterwards!

Moule, Rev'd Henry

Henry Moule, champion of the earth-closet, was born in Melksham, Wiltshire, on 27 January 1801, the sixth son of a solicitor. He went to Cambridge, and in 1829 became vicar of Fordington in Dorset, where he remained for the rest of his life.

For some years he was chaplain to the troops in Dorchester Barracks, and from the royalties of his

1845 book *Barrack sermons* he built a church at West Fordington.

In 1861 he produced a 20-page pamphlet entitled *National health and wealth, instead of the disease, nuisance, expense, and waste, caused by cess pools and water-drainage.* 'The cess-pool and privy vault are simply an unnatural abomination', he thundered, 'the water-closet ... has only increased those evils'. And he went on to describe his own amazing discovery.

First success

In the summer of 1859 he decided his cesspool was intolerable, and a nuisance to his neighbour; so he filled it in, and instructed all his family to use buckets. At first he buried the sewage in trenches in the garden, one foot deep, but he discovered by accident that in three or four weeks 'not a trace of this matter could be discovered'. So he put up a shed, sifted the dry earth beneath it, and mixed the contents of the bucket with this dry earth every morning. 'The whole operation does not take a boy more than a quarter of an hour. *And within ten minutes after its completion neither the eye nor nose can perceive anything offensive* [his italics].'

Then he discovered that he could recycle the earth, and use the same batch several times, and he began to grow lyrical. 'Water is only a vehicle for removing it out of sight and off the premises. It neither absorbs nor effectively deodorises ... The great ... agent ... is dried surface earth, both for absorption and for deodorising offensive matters.' And, he said, he no longer threw away valuable manure, but obtained a 'luxuriant growth of vegetables in my garden'.

He backed up this last point with a scientific experiment, persuading a farmer to fertilize one half of a field with earth used five times in his closet, and the other with an equal weight of super-phosphate. Swedes were planted in both halves, and those nurtured with earth manure grew one third bigger than those given only super-phosphate.

Cleanliness is next to godliness
Moule quoted a biblical precedent for his efforts, from a set of instructions about cleanliness: 'And thou shalt have a paddle upon thy weapon; and it shall be, when thou wilt ease thyself abroad, thou shalt dig therewith, and shalt turn back and cover that which cometh from thee.' (Deuteronomy 23:13). The New English Bible is even clearer: 'With your equipment you will have a

trowel, and when you squat outside, you shall scrape a hole with it and then turn and cover your excrement.'

According to Moule, doctors said that if his scheme could be generally adopted, 'much more would be effected by it for the prevention and check of disease and sickness, and for the improvement of health, than Jenner has effected by the discovery of vaccination'.

In partnership with James Bannehr, agent, he took out a patent in 1860 (No. 1316) and others in 1869 and 1873.

Moule earth-closet

He set up the Moule Patent Earth-Closet Company (Limited), which manufactured and sold an earth-closet for every occasion, the expensive models in mahogany and oak. 'They are made to act either by a handle … or self-acting, on rising from the seat. The Earth

Reservoir is calculated to hold enough for about 25 times, and where earth is scarce, or the manure required of extraordinary strength, the product may be dried as many as seven times and without losing any of its deodorising properties.'

Henry Moule died in 1880, but even in his seventies he was still trying to persuade the government that the earth-closet was the system of the future.

See also bioloos, composting lavatories, earth-closets, eco-loos, Vietnam.

Mountaineers

Mountaineers have to drink plenty of fluid to keep body systems in balance, and that fluid has to go somewhere; so several times a day they have to pee. Even for men, peeing can be difficult, in a blizzard on a slippery ice slope, through underwear, a layer or two of thermals, and a thick one-piece snowsuit. For women, the problem is much worse; they have no built-in flexible tube to carry the urine out, and exposing all to the blizzard is no fun.

The solution is the *pee-bottle, shaped, according to Everest veteran Rebecca Stephens, like a sleeping cat with no head. Kneel over it in the tent, and you never have to expose yourself to the worst of the weather. You must empty it before it freezes, but that is less of a problem. Pee-bottles are used by men, too, because they save a good deal of discomfort.

Chris Bonington

I read somewhere that the worst fate in mountaineering is to be hanging on a rope when the person on the rope above you has unstoppable diarrhoea. But defecation can go wrong even in a tent, when you are sufficiently disoriented by the altitude, as Sir Chris Bonington wrote in Everest, south west face, in 1973: 'Now that we've got these one-piece down suits, it's not so bad; in fact it's comparatively easy to relieve oneself when wearing the down suit by itself. If, however, you are wearing the down suit and the outer suit, it is absolutely desperate, trying to get the two slits in both suits lined up …' Anyway, he managed to relieve himself through one slit, but not through both. 'Pushing my left hand, which was gloved, through the sleeve, I did not realise anything was wrong—until I poked my hand through the cuff! I tried to scrape it off—rub it off—but by this time the sun had gone, it was bitterly cold and it had frozen to the consistency of concrete … Here is your dynamic leader of the British Everest Expedition, sitting at 26,000 feet feeling rather like a social pariah.'

N

NATO

NATO soldiers today are guided by STANAG 2982 on Essential Field Sanitary Requirements (STANAG is a STANdardization AGreement), which is long enough to provide latrine paper for a battalion! A typical helpful tip:

> Field sanitary appliances must be of simple design, and easily built from materials which are readily available. It is an error to predicate a method upon the salvage of a particular supply item furnishing material.

During the Gulf War of 1991, latrines took the form of steel bins lined with plastic bags, which were removed twice a day and incinerated. Separate latrines were provided for females. *See also* army, SAS.

New Zealand
At the end of the eighteenth century, according to Captain Cook, the New Zealanders had a privy for every three or four houses, which is a lot more than there were in London! The Maori word for lavatory is *whare-iti*, meaning 'the small house'.

Nightmen
In the days before main sewers were built, privies and cesspits had to be emptied regularly. Some householders did this themselves, but others summoned the 'nightmen', or 'night-soil men', who were the successors to the *gongfermors. They generally came at night, apparently to cause least disturbance in the neighbourhood, and carried the rotting sewage in buckets to their carts in the street. Often the only way to the street was through the house, which must have caused many a nightmare.

The card (*opposite*) of nightman Robert Stone—or actually a nightwoman, his daughter—shows how they had to carry the stuff in a wooden tub from the privy, visible at the bottom of the garden, through the house to their cart.

Number one hundred
On lavatory doors in some hotels in Turkey, Italy, and France, appears the label 100, rather than WC or *toilettes*. Could this be because shy English people have at some stage chalked the word 'loo' on the door? Why

Robert Stone

NIGHTMAN & RUBBISH-CARTER

At the Golden Pole the Upper End
of White Cross Street, near Old Street

N.B. Decently Performs all he Undertakes
now carried on by his Daughter

MARY BURNET.

else should *numero cento* stand for lavatory? Or could this be the origin of the word loo?

The label 100 is simpler than the Turkish word for lavatory, which is *aptesthane*, literally 'house of refuse'.

O

Optimus valve closet

The Optimus, pride and joy of plumber and writer S.S. Hellyer, was a direct development of the *Bramah. The complex mechanism was tastefully hidden in a mahogany throne, and although it probably worked better than the Bramah, the Optimus scarcely represented any great advance in technology. Hellyer wrote in 1877:

> There is no water-closet equal to a good valve-closet—perfect in all its details—especially ... for private use in good houses ... the excrement falls into about a gallon of water, and directly the closet-handle is pulled the contents of the basin (every vestige of it) are sent with some force through the closet-trap to the regions below ...

P

Pan closet

The pan closet was a sort of simplified *Bramah, in which the watertight valve was replaced by a metal pan like a saucepan, containing water. This pan sat around the bottom of the main earthenware bowl, and therefore filled the bottom few inches of it with water. After finishing, the user pulled a lever to tip the contents of the pan into the receiver below—made of cast iron or lead—and from there into the sewer. Pushing the lever back again brought the pan back up to horizontal, and it was refilled with water.

The basic idea was good. The pan provided a water seal that should have kept smells (and rats) out of the house, and the tipping mechanism was simple. The problem was that the pan had nooks and crannies that steadily became encrusted with sticky excrement. This was never flushed off, because the simple tipping action never provided enough impetus, and there was no way of getting in to clean it. So the pan closet was smelly and unhygienic.

Nevertheless, the design persisted for more than a century. William Law patented a pan closet in 1796; in 1852 it was described as being 'the common apparatus in use in first-class houses', and hundreds were still being made in the 1890s.

Paper

Most people in the West wipe themselves with paper, sometimes called loo-paper, bog-paper, bog-roll, dunny-roll, or toilet tissue. Traditionally, this used to be

newspaper. Many hours were spent on Sundays tearing pages of broadsheet into sixteen pieces, making a hole in one corner with a skewer, and tying a bundle on a loop of string, to hang from a nail in the *privy.

Bronco

With posh indoor water-closets in Victorian England came specially-made toilet paper, or bum-fodder, abbreviated to *bumf. The American company Gayety's Medicated Paper started in 1857. The British Patent Perforated Paper Company was formed to make Bronco in 1880 by Mr W.J. Alcock, who sold it from a barrow in London, and the Scott brothers in Philadelphia started making lavatory paper about the same time.

The paper, made then from esparto grass, used to be hard, shiny, and non-absorbent; Bronco came in rolls. *Jeyes began making their Hygienic Toilet Paper in 1896; it came as interleaved sheets in a flat

"Mary was so fidgety she couldn't concentrate...

...I was shocked to find that harsh toilet tissue was the cause"

Scott Tissues *Soft as Old Linen*

Reproduced by courtesy of the
Advertising Archive Limited

cardboard box. These brands went on and on; Bronco still had the lion's share of the market in the 1950s. Izal is produced today, though in small quantities. The name Bronco is still owned by Jamont, but sadly no longer used; Jamont's main brand is Dixcel, first made in Oughtibridge at the Dixon mill from the key fibre cellulose.

Since the 1960s, lavatory paper has become soft and fluffy, which is certainly much more comfortable, especially when you have a sore bottom. There is an interesting question about which is more hygienic. Hard paper must have been largely impervious to liquid and bacteria, which could not soak through to your fingers, whereas soft paper presents little barrier. However, hard paper was uncomfortable and useless for women trying to wipe themselves dry after a wee, and must often have smeared a mixture of urine and faeces over the whole area. Soft absorbent paper must be a great technological advance.

Andrex

The most popular British brand is Andrex, named after St Andrew's Mill in Walthamstow where it was invented by Ronnie Kent in 1936, although then it was only a gentlemen's hankie and sold exclusively in Harrods. Colour (pink) was introduced in 1957, but white is still the most popular colour, accounting for nearly half the total. The television commercials with a puppy began in 1972, and have frequently been voted the best adverts on telly.

On a roll

Half of all rolls sold in the UK are in four-roll packs, with 280 sheets per roll. Consumer demands led to many variations, including such environmentally friendly products as recycled paper and paper bleached without chlorine. The latest fashion seems to be *moist toilet tissue.

A 1987 survey of 227 American shoppers showed only 11.3% bought toilet paper on impulse, so 88.7% must have planned to buy it!

The annual UK lavatory paper market is worth £600 million. The amount we use is staggering. In a year, the average household uses 159 rolls; the average person uses about three quarters of a mile. If all the rolls used in Britain were unwound and laid end to end, the strip would reach further than Mars. And the average American uses more than twice as much as the average Briton.

See also eco-loos, hygiene, printed paper.

Pee-bottles

The traffic jams in Bangkok are so bad that drivers can easily get stuck on the road for six hours, and are frequently caught short in their cars. There is no easy escape on a so-called expressway. So there appeared the Comfort 1000, which is like a hospital pee-bottle and has saved many men from disaster. Unfortunately it cannot be used effectively or discreetly by women, which prompted a lively correspondence in the *Bangkok Post*. *See also* cars.

Women in church were better off than men in Victorian times. Sermons frequently lasted for several hours, and women used to take in pee-bottles, which they could use discreetly under their voluminous dresses, and so survive until the bitter end. The French name for such a vessel was a *bordaloue*, allegedly after the Jesuit priest Louis Bordaloue (1632-1704), whose sermons were bladder-strainingly long. The *bordaloue* was boat-shaped, like the *skaphion* used by Greek women since 500 BC.

See also aircraft, chamber-pots, funnels, mountaineers, RAF aircrew, urinals.

Personal space
In the West we regard excretion as something private. The only general exception to this is the men's urinal, where men pee together standing in rows.

How embarrassed are men when they have to urinate standing next to someone else? Now we know, thanks to the pioneering work of American psychologists R. Dennis Middlemist and his colleagues, who found that the nearer to being alone men are, the quicker they start peeing and the longer they go on. Having someone close by delays the start and reduces the peeing time by as much as 40%.

Piddle Valley relief
In January 1991, MP Sir James Spicer opened the new indoor lavatories for Piddle Valley First School at Piddletrenthide near Dorchester.

Pigs

Lavatories have not reached the Hmong villages, deep in the forests of western Thailand. The villagers take a morning constitutional, and squat among the bushy scrub around the village; the village pigs act as sanitary agents, collecting all the faeces.

According to Belinda Stewart Cox, who stayed there, the pigs seem to know the daily routine, and rootle around the area on spec, but also keep an eye out for likely people leaving the village, and pursue them to the chosen squatting place with a fanfare of gleeful grunts, which she found slightly embarrassing! Luckily, she found that a rice-based diet laced with chillies generally made for a speedy squat, but she suspected that for anyone inclined towards constipation the approaching crescendo of hungry and expectant hogs would act as an effective laxative.

Pigs carry out much the same function in New Guinea, Togo, and no doubt many other countries; *see* long drops. Some privies in South India are built over the pigs' trough. Every time you go, you hear the snuffling and grunting of pigs scurrying around beneath you. All deposits drop through to where they eagerly await their food.

This system used to be common in *China, but today the simplest loo there is just a naked platform, almost like a diving board with a hole, above the pig trough. You are completely exposed to passers-by. Hungry pigs wait below for what you are about to produce, and not only grunt loudly for you to get on with it, but may even jump up and snap hopefully at your bottom before you have finished!

Kjell Torstensson. From *Sanitation without water* by Uno Winblad and Wen Kilama (Macmillan, 1985)

Pissing-post

A pissing-post was a common term for a public urinal, which was a good place to stick posters and trade cards: 'whose business and good qualities you may find upon all the Pissing-posts in town' (Tom Brown, founding father of gutter journalism, 1699). In 1853 Jean Baptiste Clarières took out a patent (No. 2681) for illuminated advertising urinary columns.

See also graffiti, public lavatories, urinals.

Pit latrines

95% of the world's population have no access to a pedestal water-closet; nor are they likely to acquire enough money or enough water for such a luxury.

Up to 80% of all illness in developing countries is related to poor water supplies and sanitation. Every year, diarrhoea alone kills four million children under the age of five. One of the major concerns of such bodies as the World Health Organization, therefore, is to encourage people to develop cheap effective lavatories. The primary choice is the pit latrine; ideally one per family.

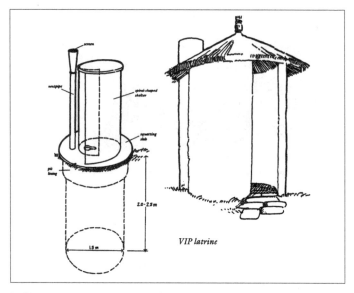

Kjell Torstensson. From *Sanitation without water* by Uno Winblad and Wen Kilama (Macmillan, 1985)

The simplest form of pit latrine is simply a deep hole in the ground with a squatting platform on top of it. The platform may be made of timber and earth, which is common in Tanzania. In Zimbabwe, however, reinforced concrete squatting slabs are used in the Ventilated Improved Pit latrines developed by the Blair Research Laboratory in Harare. The vent pipe on the sunny side of the latrine generates a draught of air down through the squat hole and up the vent pipe, which minimizes problems of smell and flies.

See also earth-closets, India, privy, Vietnam.

Praying in the privy

Sir John *Harington wrote a good deal about lavatories, including a poem with these lines about a priest who thought it was OK to pray from the throne:

A goodly Father sitting on a draught [i.e. on a loo]
To doe as need, and Nature hath us taught,
Mumbled, as was his manner, certaine prayers …

Pure prayer ascends to him that high doth sit
Downe falls the filth, for fiends of hell more fit.

Victorian *chamber-pots were decorated with all sorts of pictures and texts, including this prayer to the Roman Goddess of the lavatory:

Oh Cloacina, Goddess of this place
Look on thy servant with a smiling face.
Soft and cohesive let my offering flow—
Not rudely swift, nor obstinately slow.

See also God and Goddess, Korean monasteries, zen and the art of excretion.

Printed paper

The public loo at the river by the Houses of Parliament in London used to have smooth, shiny paper embossed or watermarked with the legend 'Property of the City of Westminster'.

Paper produced by HMSO for the Civil Service used to be hard and shiny and printed GOVERNMENT PROPERTY—NOW WASH YOUR HANDS. Now it's soft and pink!

During the Second World War, Izal produced jingoist sheets:

Hitler now screams with impatience;
Our good health is proving a strain.
May he and his Axis relations
Soon find themselves right down the drain …

More recently, loo paper has been printed with crosswords, puzzles, Happy Christmas, and rude jokes.

Privy

This used to be a general word for 'lavatory' or 'toilet' but was used especially for a shed or hut, separate from the house, which contained seats over an *earth closet, or sometimes a *water-closet. Modern dictionaries say privy is an American word for an outside lavatory, but according to the *OED*, the word privy is 600 years old, and means a private place of ease, a latrine, a necessary; hence privy house and privy stool.

A privy was the normal lavatory in Britain for people living not only in the country, but in industrial towns, until the first half of the twentieth century; it was often at the bottom of the short garden, and was called by various names—'netty' in the north-east (*see* inspiration), 'cludgie' in Glasgow.

Six-seater in Somerset—Chilthorne Domer Manor near Yeovil

Public lavatories

Public lavatories were important to the *Romans, but seemed to go out of favour in succeeding centuries. In 1358 there were apparently only four public latrines in the whole of London.

There was one on London Bridge, discharging straight into the river. However, Dick Whittington, Lord Mayor of London three times between 1397 and 1420, built at his own expense a Long House, over a tidal inlet of the Thames; a public loo with seats for 64 men on one side and 64 women on the other.

In Victorian times public lavatories began to appear in reasonable numbers in the city streets. The Public Health Act of 1848 decreed that 'public necessaries' should be provided in the interests of decency and individual comfort, but also to prevent nuisance.

Spend a penny

Flamboyant plumber George Jennings installed public lavatories for men and women at the Great Exhibition at the Crystal Palace in 1851, and although he charged a penny for their use, no fewer than 827,280 visitors seized their chance. From this historic event may come the phrase 'to spend a penny'. Mind you, charging urinators was not new; see Vespasian.

In 1927 in Berlin there were 380 urinals for men and 250 sets of water-closets, divided roughly equally between men and women, and also half first-class and half second-class. Paris boasted 3,491 urinal stalls but only 84 water-closets— 20 first-class, 51 second-class, and 13 underground. Rome had 39 sets of lavatories, with a total of about 400 water-closets; ladies were provided with a bidet and gentlemen with clothes pegs. Vienna provided some 700 water-closets and 500 urinals in 86 public conveniences.

Public loos today

A survey by G. Graham Don in 1961 roundly condemned public lavatories, especially the stall urinal; he reported on a survey among female medical students—71% thought there were too few loos for women, and only 14% preferred hot-air driers—and concluded among other things that too many (60%) of London's conveniences were underground, and that the provision for women and children was inadequate (there were four times as many for men).

A 1993 survey by Rebecca Goldsmith and her husband Selwin found that women were little better off. A handful of department stores provided more loos for women, but most public buildings were heavily biased in favour of men: e.g. British Museum 41 for men, 19 for women; Barbican Centre 54:30; Liverpool Street Station 49:20; Euston Station 42:20; Royal Festival Hall 64:28; MGM cinema, Fulham 8:2.

The Women's Design Service suggest women suffer from both inadequate provision of public lavatories, and their poor design, and have published a handbook on the design of women's public toilets, entitled *At women's convenience*. They produce some interesting statistics; because women usually sit down, they spend on average 80 seconds using a public toilet, while men spend only 45 seconds.

Recommended loos

In 1993 there appeared in Westbourne Grove, London W2, a splendiferous public lavatory designed by Piers Gough and made a reality by John Scott, property developer, art-deco-fancier, and pillar of the local conservation society. The exterior is shaped like a flat-iron, and cunningly planned to follow the triangle of

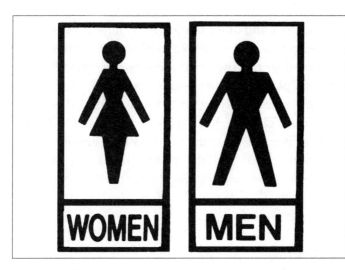

the traffic island, and the Daily Telegraph hailed the innovative structure as 'the best lavatory in the world'.

Among other highly recommended loos are at Mothercare in Oxford Street, the Grosvenor Wing of St George's Hospital, Tooting, the London Library in St James's Square, and the Wallace Collection in Manchester Square. *See also* Amerdale House, Blandford House, converted loos.

R

RAF aircrew
In the early days, RAF aircrew were supplied with *chemical lavatories, so when the Dambusters went, they went on Elsans. Modern versions are still used in Hercules transport aircraft.

Tornadoes and other fast jets don't have time or space for the pilots and other aircrew to use conventional lavatories; so they pee into a disposable 'piddle-pack'. This is a plastic bag like a colostomy bag, strapped to the leg inside the flying suit, which is rubberized like a wet-suit. The bag has a plastic valve, and a sponge inside to prevent the urine from sloshing about.

Both the RAF and the USAF are having to think fast about providing for the female pilots coming into service.

See also aircraft.

Right stuff

The first American astronaut was Alan Sheppard. The embarrassing story of his first flight, on 5 May 1961, is told by Tom Wolfe in his book *The right stuff.*

Sheppard was woken early, checked by the astronauts' doctor, and given breakfast. His body was covered with biosensors, including a thermometer in the rectum. Then he struggled into his spacesuit, and was finally 'inserted' into the Mercury capsule on top of a huge Redstone rocket at Cape Canaveral—and it was still an hour before dawn.

He lay on his back as though in an armchair tilted backwards, but in such a small space that he could barely move his arms; everything else was fixed. He was facing straight up into the sky, but could see nothing, for he had no window; they had been designed but not yet made. The nation waited for the launch with baited breath, glued to their radios and television sets.

His flight was scheduled to last only 15 minutes; so no provision was made for excretion. Unfortunately the countdown was held up again and again by minor technical problems, until he had been lying there for more than four hours; eventually the pressure of the urine in his bladder became unbearable.

What could he do? To get out of the capsule would have taken perhaps an hour, and seriously interrupted the countdown. He did not want to postpone the flight; what would they say on radio and TV? Inside, however, he had nothing to pee into, and no room to manoeuvre; in any case there was no way to get the urine out through his spacesuit.

On the closed-circuit radio he warned mission control. There was a tense delay for frenzied discussion—the danger was that the urine would cause an electrical short, which in the capsule's atmosphere of pure oxygen could start a fire—and then permission came back to go ahead and do it in the suit.

The warm stream trickled over his stomach and round his waist. It knocked out a couple of biosensors, but did no serious damage. It ended up as a pool in the small of his back. With that cooling pool of urine he completed the mission and immediately became a national hero, earning a medal from President John F. Kennedy and a tickertape parade on Broadway.

Roadside lavatories

In 1966 the Advisory Council on Public Sanitation issued a blistering report on roadside loos; their research team found a lavatory 'of sorts' at least every five miles, but more than 70% of all garage lavatories were either foul or inadequate, as were 74% of cafe lavatories. They were not surprised to find that 'so many lay-bys were fouled'.

By 1992 the AA found little improvement. There were no service stations on the M40, the M11, the M20, or the M23. The M25, one of the busiest roads in the UK, had only one service station in 117 miles to cope with 150,000 vehicles a day. A driver going from Birmingham to Kent on the M40, M25, and M20 could travel 155 miles without seeing a toilet.

See also cars, pee-bottles.

Romans

The Romans built public baths all over the place, and they also built lavatories; we know because many still exist.

Housesteads

In AD 122, after the visit of the Emperor Hadrian, the Romans constructed a defensive wall 74 miles long, right across northern England, in order to keep out the warmongering tribes from the north. This came to be called Hadrian's Wall. One of the major forts along the wall was at Housesteads, which must have been the base for about 800 soldiers, and the troops shared a single communal lavatory, in the south-east corner of the fort.

The latrine was a room about 10m x 5m, and had a single wooden bench seat round three walls, with about 20 holes; the sitters faced inwards, with their backs to the walls. There were no partitions; they seem to have regarded using the lavatory as a communal experience.

The wooden seat was built over a trench, through which diverted river water flowed continuously in an anticlockwise direction, and since the lavatory is at the downhill end of the site, the sewage was carried straight out through the wall of the fort—and was probably used as fertilizer. Rainwater was collected in a cistern for use in dry weather.

Bum sponges

In front of the sitters—just beyond their feet—was a shallow channel or gutter which also held running water. To wipe their bottoms, Romans generally used sponges on sticks, which they rinsed in this channel by their feet. The thought of using such a sponge immediately after someone else is horrible—the sponges must have been fertile breeding grounds for bacteria—and it seems likely that each man had his own sponge, which he carried with him. However, sponges can't have been readily available in northern Britain, and the remains of moss have been found in some sites; so a handful of moss was probably an alternative to the sponge. This may have provided a less satisfactory wipe, but at least it was disposable, and used only once.

In the crucifixion story in the Bible, a Roman soldier is said to have offered Jesus a drink from a sponge soaked in vinegar. This is mentioned in all four gospels; for example Matthew 27:48 (Authorized version) '... one of them ... took a sponge, and filled it with vinegar, and put it on a reed, and gave him to drink'. Luke 23:36 has 'And the soldiers also mocked him, coming to him, and offering him vinegar'. The gesture seems more likely to have been an insult than compassionate; Roman soldiers carried only one kind of sponge, and to rub it in the face of a victim would have been an obvious cheap joke.

Rome

A few grand houses in Rome had their own private lavatories. Some of these were flushed with water, but most were just simple seats over a tub, or over a drain to the cesspit in the cellar or back yard. However, most people used public lavatories—which must have simplified both water supply and sewage disposal—and some of the lavatories were very public; indeed they were places to meet and gossip.

Rome in AD 315 boasted 144 public loos, most of which accommodated many people. At the Roman outpost of Timgad in North Africa, there was a public lavatory for every 28 people; probably more than we have anywhere today. Sir Mortimer Wheeler describes the forum there as a large paved rectangular space, with the town hall on one side, a temple on another. On a third side was a public lavatory; rows of stone seats with holes in pairs, divided by armrests carved in the shape of dolphins. There were no walls or partitions; the sitters would have been in full view of the hustle and bustle of the market place.

Lepcis Magna

At Lepcis Magna, also in North Africa, the great baths included two huge lavatories, in each of which 30 or 40 people sat on marble seats on three sides of the room, watched by a statue on the fourth. Lavatories were often built with public baths, so that part of the waste water from the baths could be diverted into a channel underneath the seats, to flush the effluent into the main sewer. This simple design was effective for hundreds of years, and was used all over the Roman empire.

Royal Navy

In Nelson's navy the 'heads' for the lower ranks were simply holes in a wooden plank or planks projecting in front of the bows beside the figurehead; often, on small ships, dangerously close to the waterline. The excrement fell straight into the sea, and was carried away by the bow wave.

If the users were unlucky and the waves were rough, a good deal of sea came up through the holes. On ships as big as the *Victory* the heads were safer because they were high above the waterline.

The lavatories were called 'heads' because the whole of the front of the ship is called the head. A rival theory that the sitter shouted 'heads' to warn anyone below not to stick their head out of a porthole seems highly unlikely; there are never portholes in the extreme bows.

Modern navy loos

All modern navy ships rely on 'collect, hold, and transfer', using either a vacuum system, or a biological system. The vacuum systems are the same as on commercial ships; they use a small (1.2 litre) fresh-water flush, mainly to refill the bowl. The effluent is removed by the vacuum from below and transferred to the holding tanks—usually two or three per ship.

Royalty

Edmund II of England, son of Ethelred the Unready and known as Edmund Ironside, was allegedly murdered in his privy in AD 1016; Canute then became King of all England. Also trapped in the same situation was James I of Scotland, who was killed in his privy by rebel nobles in 1437. *See also* death.

Elizabeth I had the second Ajax water-closet in 1596 (*see* Harington), while at Hampton Court, Henry VIII's courtiers used a communal privy called the Great House of Easement (*see* history), but Henry VIII himself preferred a *close stool—a box sumptuously upholstered in black velvet with ribbons and fringes, and 2,000 gold nails, and containing a pewter pot. He was attended by the Groom of the Stool; a privileged position given to a high-ranking courtier. One night in 1539 Henry took laxative pills and an enema, and the groom recorded that he slept until 2 a.m., 'when His Grace rose to go upon his stool which, with the working of the pills and the enema … had a very fair siege'. *See also* Acton Court.

James I of England (1566-1625) used to hunt all day, and never left the saddle for anything. At home, he had a richly-chased silver chamber-pot.

Charles V of Spain was born in a privy, whereas in 1760 George II of England died on his water-closet.

George IV is said to have used a portable water-closet; a round metal basin flushed by a force-pump through an open hole in the bottom into a large metal container below. He is also said to have died on his chamber-pot.

At Windsor about 1710 Queen Anne had a 'little place with a seat of casement of marble with sluices of water to wash all down', yet 150 years later Queen Victoria used an earth-closet there. In 1844, worried about the number of sore throats and unexplained fevers among the servants at Windsor Castle, Prince Albert ordered a survey, and found 53 cesspools, some centuries old and many overflowing, under the castle itself.

Queen Victoria was once being shown round Cambridge University, where the town sewers discharged straight into the River Cam. She turned to her guide, Dr Whewell, Master of Trinity, and asked what were all the pieces of paper floating in the river. As cool as a cucumber, he replied 'Those, ma'am, are notices that bathing is forbidden.'

Royal loo seats were allegedly carved into presentation cigarette boxes; *see Britannia*. After Queen Alexandra had paid a royal visit to the heads in a naval establishment, an enterprising rating apparently rushed in, removed the seat, and framed it with a tasteful caption.

Queen Elizabeth II was crowned in Westminster Abbey on 6 June 1953. The coronation ceremony took two hours, and was attended by many elderly dignitaries, some of whom had been there for up to five hours in advance, and were bound to want to relieve themselves during the proceedings. According to Pudney, neatly concealed by the steps of the altar were 213 chemical closets.

S

SAS

In his book about an SAS operation in the 1991 Gulf War, Andy McNab explains how important it was for his team of eight to hide their excrement. SOP—Standard Operation Procedure—was to collect all their urine in a plastic one-gallon petrol container. When it was full one of them would carry it at least 2km away into the bush, move a rock, dig a hole underneath it, empty the can, and replace the earth and rock. This would prevent detection by smell, animal interest, or insect activity.

They squatted to shit into plastic bags, which they knotted and carried in their rucksacks for later disposal. They could not afford to have the enemy find and analyse their faeces to discover where they had come from and what they were eating. (*See also* bottom of the world, Iraqi cubicle.)

S-bend or u-bend

Sewer gases smell horrible, and are toxic and inflammable; they can carry both diseases and the risk of explosion.

They are kept at bay by the water in the s-bend or u-bend, which is important, and tremendously clever, although far from new; in his 1775 patent *Cumming said it was 'too well known to require a description here'.

All modern water-closets have an s-bend, which forms a water-trap or seal. British Standard 7358 requires a water seal with a minimum depth of 50mm. Every time the lavatory is flushed, the contents are removed, and the s-bend fills with clean water—at least, this should be the case.

To prevent gas bubbling up through the water trap, the vent pipe relieves any excess pressure at roof level.

Scouts

In *Scouting for boys*, Robert Baden-Powell wrote 'On reaching the camping ground the latrine is the very first thing to attend to ... The trench should be two feet deep, three feet long, and one foot wide, so that the user can squat astride of it, one foot on each side. A sprinkling of earth should be thrown in after use ...' These instructions are similar to those issued to the *army—which is presumably where he got them from.

He also had strong views on regularity: '... to be healthy and strong, you must keep your blood healthy and clean inside you. This is done by breathing in lots of pure, fresh air ... and ... by having a "rear" daily, without fail ... If there is any difficulty about it one day, drink plenty of water, especially before and just after breakfast, and practise body-twisting exercises, and all should be well.'

Seats

Lavatory seats of marble and limestone have survived for thousands of years; wood has surely been used for

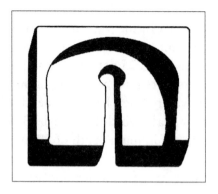

at least as long, even though it does not last. The stone seats must have been cold on the fundament, unless they were somehow upholstered, or the users were able to arrange folds of clothing under their buttocks.

Materials

At the city of Akhenaten in Egypt in 1350 BC some lavatories had limestone seats like the later Roman ones; other people seem to have preferred wood.

Henry VIII and later monarchs used *close stools with padded seats covered with velvet; *see* royalty. Dr Johnson would have disapproved; he said firmly to Boswell 'there is nothing so good as the plain board'.

Plastic seats became cheap and therefore common in the 1960s. People have claimed they are hygienic, because the hard plastic surface should be inhospitable to bacteria; *see* hygiene.

Comfort

Americans seem to regard a hygienic seat as almost indispensable; in Thomas Harris's horrific thriller *The Silence of the Lambs*, arch-villain Hannibal Lecter is detained in a secure hospital cell, and one of the direst threats by his unpleasant jailer Dr Chilton is to take away his toilet seat if he behaves badly.

We in the West are used to single seats, but a few decades ago, multi-seater privies were common. The *Romans had multi-seater public lavatories, often just a dozen holes cut two feet apart in a single plank of wood. There is, in the Science Museum in London, a two-holer corner seat from a lavatory at Strutt's Mill in Derbyshire, where they had innovative locks on the loo doors! Family two- and three-holers were normal; there is a well-preserved six-holer at Chilthome Domer Manor.

The shape of the seat has a dramatic effect on the style and elegance of the lavatory, as well as on the comfort of the user. I have always enjoyed using Victorian lavatories where the seat was a whole shelf, perhaps two feet wide and three feet long, often with a matching lid that covered all. The traditional Roman seat seems to have been keyhole-shaped, with a much narrower hole than we use today.

The British Standard

British Standards 1254, 5503, and 7358 are firm on seats. The minimum width of the opening must be 215mm and the minimum length 255mm. (These got smaller between 1977 and 1981; perhaps we are getting more accurate?)

The height from the floor to the top of the seat must be between 405 and 435mm. At its thickest the seat must be at least 19mm thick. The inside edges must overlap the inside bottom edge of the flushing rim by 5mm, and the seat when raised shall not fall forward. I know of several office lavatories with seats that fall forward. Next time I come across one I shall send a note to the boss, pointing out that this contravenes BS 7358!

[It's for our biggest customer!]

CHURCH *Seat* SEATS

Reprduced courtesy of the
Advertising Archive Limited

The divided seat

Men often have difficulty in peeing with absolute precision, and therefore often drip on the seat when trying to pee through it. The traditional response to this has been either a divided seat, with a gap at the front, which goes back into prehistory and survives in many school lavatories today, or a hinged seat that a male user lifts when he wants to pee standing, and everyone puts down before sitting.

Beyond the Fringe

A common sign in lavatories on trains, was GENTLEMEN PLEASE LIFT THE SEAT. Perhaps lower classes were not expected to carry out this complex operation! In his trouser-monologue during the 1961 satirical revue *Beyond the Fringe*, Jonathan Miller made some more detailed suggestions:

> that marvellous, unpunctuated motto over lavatories saying GENTLEMEN LIFT THE SEAT. What exactly does it mean? Is it a sociological description—a definition of a gentleman which I can either take or leave? Or perhaps it's a Loyal Toast? It could be a blunt military order ... or an invitation to upper-class larceny ...

Automatic seats

In the 1860s appeared 'self-rising closet seats'—wooden seats with counterweights at the back so that when the user stood up the seat rose too. These were popular for 50 years or more, but went out of fashion again, perhaps because they had a tendency to move too quickly, and smack the bottom of the riser.

Another popular device was the lavatory that flushed automatically when the sitter stood up. John Ashley patented one in 1792; Thomas *Crapper another 99 years later, and there were many in between.

See also Japan, lighting-up loo.

Sense

'Sense' is the name of a sculpture in the Icon Gallery in Birmingham; it is a representation of a giant lavatory. *See also* Duchamp.

Sewer

Sewers are pipes or channels for carrying sewage from lavatories to places where it can be dealt with, most often sewage treatment works or sewage farms. Sewers also carry rainwater and other waste water.

The oldest-known sewer, at Mohenjo-Daro in the Indus Valley, was built about 2500 BC. The *Romans built extensive sewers in their cities—there was a network of sewers under the military base at Eboracum, now known as York—and because the Latin for sewer was *cloaca* they called the biggest sewer in Rome *cloaca maxima*.

Underground sewers were reinvented in Hamburg in 1843, and after the Great Stink in London in 1858 the idea caught on in England.

See also history.

Shaw, George Bernard

Shaw (1856-1950), Irish dramatist and writer, lived in London from 1876, and championed many causes, including feminism. In 1927 he wrote,

> When I went into active municipal life, and became a member of the health committee of a London borough council (St Pancras) the question of providing accommodation for women was one which I conceived to be pressingly important. And you can have no idea of the difficulty I had in getting that notion, to a limited extent, into the heads of the gentlemen who were working with me on the committee …
>
> I talked and talked to get proper sanitary accommodation for women, I found it impossible for a long time to get over the opposition to it as an indecency. A lavatory for women was described as an abomination.

The only memorial to this great struggle of George Bernard Shaw's is the ladies under the traffic island in the middle of Parkway, at its junction with Camden High Street.

See also public lavatories, urinettes.

Signs

Lavatories have always been fertile ground for signs. Public loos advertise their presence with such helpful labels as TOILETS, LADIES, GENTLEMEN (or GENTS), and PUBLIC CONVENIENCES. This idea is far from new; the Bible commands it: 'You shall have a sign outside the camp showing where you can withdraw.' (New English Bible, Deuteronomy 23:12.)

According to the magazine *Private Eye*, the Cheltenham Spa town council voted to change the signs in Cheltenham from MEN and WOMEN to LADIES and GENTLEMEN in order 'to attract a better class of person'.

Travellers have often been confused by foreign equivalents; for example in Germany HERREN was often taken to mean LADIES. Now, fortunately, most such signs have been replaced by symbols. Home-made signs are sometimes seen in the gents in pubs: WE AIM TO PLEASE— YOU AIM TOO, PLEASE.

Siphonic action

The ordinary domestic lavatory has one or two siphons. In the UK, the cistern houses a siphonic flush; *see* flushing.

There may also be a siphon in the pan if it is emptied by double-trap siphonic action. A siphonic-emptying closet was patented by John Gray in 1855 (No. 2091), and a double-trap siphon by John Randall Mann in 1870 (No. 577). An American version was patented as the pneumatic closet by Jas E. Boyle in 1882. It was used in expensive lavatories in the early part of this century, and became fashionable in the UK in the 1960s and '70s; if you are lucky enough to use an old lavatory you may find it has wondrously efficient siphonic emptying.

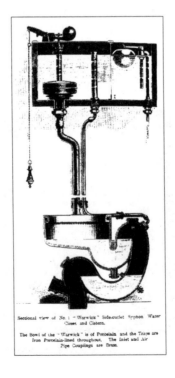

Sectional view of No. 1 " Warwick " Side-outlet Syphon Water Closet and Cistern.

The Bowl of the " Warwick " is of Porcelain and the Traps are Iron Porcelain-lined throughout. The Inlet and Air Pipe Couplings are Brass.

Hardly has the water begun to flow into the pan than all its contents disappear round the s-bend with a *whoosh*. Only afterwards does the pan fill up again.

This siphonic action is caused by having two *s-bend water traps, with an air space between them. A tube connects this air space to the main flush delivery pipe. When you flush, the rush of water in this pipe lowers the pressure in the tube (by the Bernouilli effect). This pulls some of the air out of the air space, and the normal air pressure in the pan drives all its contents round the first bend. In other words, the contents of the pan are sucked down before the flush arrives.

Slop-closet or tipper-closet

The automatic slop-water closet, or tipper-closet, had a self-acting tipper which was filled with used bathwater or washing-up water. When full, it overbalanced, and the soapy water rushed down a pipe and flushed the lavatory, which could be some distance away; for example in a privy out in the yard. Some were still in use in the 1980s, and children remember them because of the sudden spooky underground roar when the monster flushed.

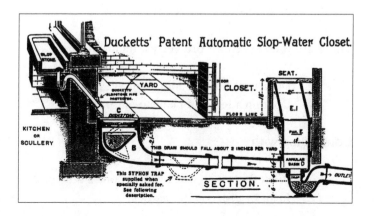

John Aubrey was probably describing a tipper in 1718 when he wrote of 'a pretty machine to cleanse a House of Office, viz, by a small stream of water no bigger than one's finger, which ran into an engine made like a bit of a fire-shovel, which hung upon its centre of gravity, so that when it was full a considerable quantity of water fell down with some force'.

Smallest room

The loo is sometimes called the smallest room in the house, but if you really want to try a small one, pay a visit to the downstairs gents in the Queen's Head in Stockport, which is just 17 inches wide—the whole room, that is! One 25-stone customer got completely jammed inside, and had to be rescued with soap by the fire brigade.

Songs

There have been many lavatorial songs, not to mention formal chants (*see* Korean monasteries). Here are two well-known examples:

> *Chorus* What do you do, if you want to do a poo
> In an English country garden?
> Take down your pants, and suffocate the ants
> In an English country garden.

There are then several more verses, including:

> Dig a little hole, and do a sausage roll ...
> Do it on a log, and blame it on the dog ...

Concluding with:

> What do you do when you've done a little poo
> In an English country garden?

> Pick up a leaf and wipe your underneath
> In an English country garden.

Another children's favourite is:

> Oh dear! What can the matter be?
> Three old ladies stuck [or locked] in the
>   lavatory.
> They were there from Monday to Saturday;
> Nobody knew they were there.

Squatting

For the human body trying to defecate, squatting is a much better attitude than sitting. Sitting on a seat leaning forward with the weight resting on the thighs makes a sharp angle—almost a kink—between the rectum and the anus. Faeces have to change direction, and the more they are pushed, the worse the angle gets.

In a squatting position, with the heels under the hips, the rectum is almost vertical, and in a straight line with the anus. The muscles all work together, with gravity, to assist defecation.

One result of this is that constipation is much more common in rich countries where people sit, than in poor countries where they squat.

See also constipation.

Starship Enterprise

I am told by Trekkies that the crew of the original Starship Enterprise never visited the lavatory—or at least were never seen to go during three decades of five-year missions. Furthermore, the official plans of the spacecraft, I am told, revealed no sign of lavatorial facilities. If this is true, the crew must have had their legs crossed for a long time! What a nightmare—nowhere to boldly go …

However, I am relieved (as are the crew, I expect) to say that the Star Fleet Technical Manual shows the presence of those unseen lavatories. Each single stateroom has a shared *en suite* bathroom with loo (and Jacuzzi!), each double stateroom has an *en suite* bathroom with two water-closets. And there is a toilet adjacent to the main bridge, just behind and to the right of the screens of the command module. There are even toilets in the detention cells in the security section.

However, this was published much later, and maybe, just maybe, the original plans did lack lavatories.

Submariners

There is a basic problem with lavatories in a submarine; how do you get the sewage out without letting the sea in?

Polaris nuclear submarines had a crew of 136, and stayed under water for a month or more. They had a dozen lavatories, six together in the main quarters, the others scattered elsewhere for officers, the bridge, and so on.

The lavatories themselves were housed in cubicles, and looked more or less like conventional lavatories, but each one had a ball-valve below the bowl. Having finished, the user opened the valve to let the contents out, then opened the flushing valve to flush the bowl with sea water from a tank inside the hull, then closed both valves.

All the sewage was collected in large 'sanitary tanks' in the bottom of the submarine. When these were nearly full they were discharged. 'Blowing the sanitary tanks' was a slightly tricky process. First the officers made sure there was no danger of detection by hostiles—they avoided discharging in enemy territory—next they pressurized the main holding tanks to just above the exterior sea pressure; then they opened the valve to blow the sewage into the sea. They were careful never to empty the tanks completely, since that would have released bubbles, which might have given them away. Then the pressurized air remaining in the tanks was released into the submarine through a charcoal filter to remove the smell.

Superloos

In the 1970s, the notorious old *pissoirs* on the pavements of Paris were becoming both expensive to maintain and socially unacceptable. Because of the growing problems of vandalism, the authorities approached Jean-Claude Decaux, a successful designer of bus stops and other street furniture. Could he design an attractive, vandal-proof, low-maintenance public lavatory?

His solution was the superloo, or Automatic Public Convenience, to give it its proper name. APCs are now springing up not only in Paris and London but all over Europe.

The door opens automatically when you put a coin in the slot (in England usually 10p or 20p). Once you are inside—it knows, because of your weight on the floor—the door swings shut and locks behind you. You can easily open the door from the inside at any time, and if you fail to do so it opens automatically after 17 minutes.

The wash-basin is set into the wall, and fully automated; just put your hands in for soap and water, followed in due course by warm air for drying.

When you have finished, opened the door, and left,

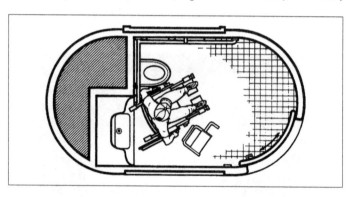

the lavatory bowl retracts into the wall compartment, where it is spray-cleaned, disinfected, and air-dried. Meanwhile the floor is sprayed clean.

Swift, Jonathan

Jonathan Swift was a satirist, poet, and Anglican cleric. Born in Dublin in 1667, he lived partly in London and partly in Dublin, where in 1713 he was made Dean of St Patrick's. There he wrote *Gulliver's Travels* (1726).

In 1729 he built two privies—one for men and one for women—for his friend Lady Acheson: '... In sep'rate cells the He's and She's Here pay their vows with bended knees ...'

He also wrote a whole book about sewage, with the catchy title *Human Ordure*. He was strongly against chamber-pots, and wrote in a pamphlet of 'Directions to servants' (1745)—note that 'to pluck a Rose' means to relieve themselves.

I am very much offended with those Ladies, who are so proud and lazy, that they will not be at the Pains of stepping into the Garden to pluck a Rose, but keep an odious Implement, sometimes in the Bed-chamber itself, or at least in a dark Closet adjoining, which they make Use of to ease their worst Necessities; and, you are the usual Carriers away of the Pan, which maketh not only the Chamber, but even their Cloaths offensive, to all who come near.

T

Thunder-box

The thunder-box was the traditional lavatory for the British army and other ex-pats in exile in India and Africa. Often made from an upturned tea-chest with a hole cut in the bottom and a container inside, it was like a military *close stool.

The *Sword of Honour* trilogy by Evelyn Waugh (1903-66) opens with *Men at Arms*. In it, Waugh tells the story of the absurd and eccentric Apthorpe, who joins his regiment carrying a 'large square object',

which at first he refuses to discuss but soon admits with pride is his own thunder-box: 'He opened it, showing a mechanism of heavy cast-brass and patterned earthenware of solid Edwardian workmanship. On the inside of the lid was a plaque bearing the embossed title of Connelly's Chemical Closet.' (Reproduced by permission of Chapman & Hall Ltd.)

Toilet training

In the West, babies wear nappies or diapers until they learn to use a potty. For many parents, the process of teaching a child to use the pot becomes a battleground. According to expert Dr Penelope Leach, many babies at one year will be thoroughly experienced in sitting on pots, while others will never have met a pot in their lives. She points out that the child has nothing to gain from performing on the pot, except praise.

There are both physiological and psychological fences; young babies cannot learn to use a pot for various reasons. First, their nerves are not well enough developed for them to know when they have excreted, let alone when they are ready to do so. Second, they do not know how to control the performance; the instructions to the sphincters are not yet connected up.

Many clever devices are sold to worried mothers; for example a musical potty that sings the toddler's praises; gold plated sensors register moisture in the potty, triggering one of 16 cheerful tunes, including 'Yankee Doodle', 'Little Brown Jug', and 'Chim-Chim-Cheree'. Make toilet training fast, easy, and fun!

See also China.

Trains

Railways were providing seriously useful transport by the middle of the nineteenth century. As people travelled greater distances, they needed to relieve themselves en route; nothing can make someone more desperate than being stuck in a crowded train with a bursting bladder or a bloated bowel. To begin with, passengers had to leap out when the train stopped at a station, and hope they could fight their way into the small station lavatories and out again in time to get back on the train before it left.

The spectacle became common of all the men running to one end of the train and peeing off the end of the platform, while all the ladies went to the other and attempted to relieve themselves decorously under their long skirts, perhaps using *pee-bottles, while ostensibly admiring the view.

The Great Western
When the Great Western Railway opened in the 1840s, every train between London and Bath was required to stop only at Swindon, where they changed engines, and for only 10 minutes. The journey took four hours; so by Swindon, many of the passengers were desperate, and the queues for the inadequate facilities must have been absurd, particularly as they had to try to get something to eat in the same 10 minutes.

Marked with a 'z'
Holiday trains from Burton to Skegness made a special loo stop at Sleaford until the 1920s; such special stops were marked with a 'z' in the timetable.

The South Eastern
About 1850 Richard Mansell designed a sumptuous royal saloon for the South Eastern Railway. In the 'ante-room' was an upholstered seat concealing a 'patent convenience'. This may have been only a *close stool, but in 1860 the SER's invalid saloon boasted a portable water-closet, which may have been the same thing. This WC had a round metal basin with a hole but no valve in the bottom, and a big metal container underneath. It was flushed by a force-pump in a small cistern on one side. Similar contraptions were used on Thames river steamers.

The London and North Western
In May 1850 the LNWR had an invalid carriage with a water-closet, which was perhaps of similar design. What is amazing is that even though they recognized the problem and had the solution, the companies waited about 30 years before providing lavatories for ordinary people.

Some LNWR first-class compartments apparently had commodes built into what looked like ordinary seats, but the smell must have been unpleasant.

Corridors
Detailed designs for corridor trains with lavatories were made in the 1860s by William Bridges Adams, but he was dismissed as a crank. In 1873 sleeping cars acquired lavatories, but not until the 1880s did lavatories appear regularly on ordinary trains. These were trains without corridors, and one common arrangement was for a toilet compartment to be sandwiched and shared between two passenger compartments. Even these were mainly for first-class passengers; the first lavatory for third-class passengers was probably installed in 1886.

The first recorded corridor on a train was provided for Queen Victoria in 1869, although it is said she would not use it when the train was moving! In 1882 the Great Northern Railway introduced the first British side-corridors. There was a Ladies at one end of the carriage and a Gents at the other, but no way of getting to the next carriage. However, corridor trains were not generally introduced until the 1890s.

Please do not use lavatory when train is at a station

Press lever to flush

Train lavatories always discharged straight on to the track, which is why they display notices telling you not to flush the toilet in stations; they don't want unpleasant heaps in sight of waiting passengers.

The USA
American railway companies were much quicker to recognize the importance of the lavatory, which was sometimes called the lavatory, but more often the saloon, dressing room, water-closet, washroom, retiring room, or loafing room. Before the 1880s they were airless cupboards, often only three feet square, containing only a primitive dry hopper with a hole directly over the

track. But they appeared on trains, especially those of the Philadelphia and Columbia Railroad, by the late 1830s, and were probably common by the early 1840s, which was about 40 years earlier than in Britain. By the 1880s ordinary American coaches had separate washing facilities for men and women; some luxury cars had bathtubs, and one inventor dreamed up a three-compartment bathing car modelled on a fully equipped Turkish bath.

Tree-loo

During the early 1980s there was a good deal of fighting around the small bush town of Katima Mulilo, on the Zambezi River, about 60 miles upstream from the Victoria Falls. The South West African Police Force (SWAPF) had a lot of people on the beat, and they needed somewhere to relieve themselves outside the police station, since going inside meant penetrating several layers of security, which wasted a lot of time.

Across the dusty road from the police station was a large baobab tree, and they built themselves a lavatory inside it! Local craftsmen cut a small room in the huge trunk, and fitted it out with not only a proper flushing water-closet but also an overhead light and a lockable steel door which kept the lavatory exclusive for SWAPF.

Trough closet

About 1860 Ducketts, Crapper, and others produced closets that were simply metal troughs edged with hardwood rails, on which people could presumably sit with discomfort. They came in two standard lengths— 12 feet and 24 feet—and were intended for communal use in factories and schools. For those with spare cash or sensitive bottoms, optional extras of hinged or fixed seats were available.

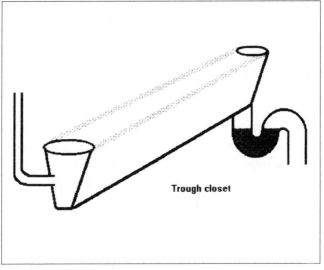

Trough closet

U

United States

Americans have their own *euphemisms; they rarely use the word toilet, and never call it a lavatory. In the home it's a can, crapper, john, washroom, or most often a bathroom; they will even say 'Hey! The cat just went to the bathroom on the table!'

The origins of many of these terms are not clear. One suggestion is that the word john might have come from the Rev'd Edward Johns, who in 1867 bought a pottery in England; *see* how to make a loo. He won an award at the Philadelphia Exhibition in 1876, and Americans began importing his products; 'We get our Johns direct from England.' However, a Harvard University regulation of 1735 declared 'No Freshman shall go to the Fellows' John'—and this was 132 years before Edward Johns entered the business.

Another possibility is Sir John *Harington, who made a pioneering water-closet a generation before the Pilgrim Fathers sailed. Likewise the word crapper may or may not have come from Thomas *Crapper.

Rest room

Public lavatories are called rest rooms or comfort stations; on *trains they used to be saloons, loafing rooms, dressing rooms, or retiring rooms, and NASA has waste management and waste collection systems; *see* astronauts.

Privies

Privy construction is brilliantly described by Charles Sale.

Longfellow
Henry Wadsworth Longfellow installed a water-closet in his New England home in 1840, and caused widespread local interest.

The American loo
In the mid-nineteenth century, Americans either imported lavatories or followed UK and other foreign designs, but in 1876 William Smith of San Francisco patented a special jet to clear the bowl, and in 1882 Jas E. Boyle patented the double-trap siphon. After that the US Patent Office was deluged with new American designs, and the British and American systems began to diverge.

The *pan closet gave way to the hopper and the wash-out, and today the most popular design in the United States is probably the *wash-out closet with double-trap *siphonic action. American cisterns have flapper valves where the British use siphons; *see* flushing.

Urinals

The word urinal means three things: either a glass vessel or *chamber-pot for urine, especially for an incontinent or bedridden person; a fixed receptacle for urination; or a room or building containing such receptacles. The word urinal comes from the Latin, but was being used in Britain by the thirteenth century. The pronunciation is either yuRInal or YOURinal.

Jordans

By the fourteenth century the Latin word *jurdanus* was becoming common, and this seems to have become the English word jordan. There is a suggestion that jordan is short for Jordan-bottle—originally a bottle of water brought from the river Jordan by crusaders or pilgrims—but this is doubtful.

The jordan was often a glass vessel or phial that could be used for medical examination of the urine. In the middle of the seventeenth century, jordans were often called 'looking glasses', perhaps because the doctor looked into them to inspect the urine. John Collop wrote:

> Hence looking-glasses, chamber pots we call,
> 'Cause in your pisse we can discover all.

In 1382 Roger Clerk of Wandsworth, convicted of pretending to have medical and prophetic knowledge, was sentenced to ride through London, facing the horse's tail, with two jordans hung round his neck.

In his English-Latin phrase book of 1519, William Horman gives the useful phrase 'See that I lacke nat by my beddis syde a chayer of easement: with a vessell under: and a urnall bye.'

Chaucer wrote about jordans— 'thyne urynals and thy Iurdones'—and so did Shakespeare; two carriers are complaining about their lodgings in *Henry IV* part one, II, 18: 'Why, they will allow us ne'er a jordan; and then we leak in the chimney ...'

See also chamber-pots, France, pee-bottles, public lavatories.

Urinette

In 1927, concerned that women were poorly provided with public lavatories, and always had to pay to use a cubicle, while men could use urinals without charge, the Public Health Committee in London reported that 'a fitment for women has been designed, known as a urinette. It is similar to a w.c., but is narrower and has a flushing rim ... Urinettes are fixed in w.c. compartments, usually with a curtain in front instead of a door.'

Eight boroughs installed urinettes in a total of 30 places, but, the report confesses, 'The urinettes are not popular ... the attendants state that they are sometimes used in an uncleanly manner and require supervision to maintain them in a hygienic condition'.

See also Shaw.

V

Vespasian

There was a considerable Roman trade in urine, which was collected in pots on street corners and used for stiffening and dyeing cloth. The Emperor Vespasian (AD 69-79) imposed a tax on the use of public urinals, which became known as Vespasiani. When one of his sons complained about the tax, the Emperor held up a coin, and asked 'Does it smell?' Later the *pissoirs* in *France were called Vespasiennes in his honour!

According to Suetonius, the court jester said of Vespasian's miserable expression that even when he was at his merriest he looked 'as if he had been wringing hard on a close stool'.

Vietnam

In the late 1950s the people of Quang Ngai Province in Vietnam responded to government initiative by developing a double-vault latrine. These are built above ground, at least 10 metres away from houses, where possible. For about two months the family uses vault one, covering each deposit with a sprinkling of ashes or dry earth. Urine is collected in a separate pot; so the vault remains fairly dry.

Meanwhile vault two is sealed with a lid on top. After two months the old excrement, now turned to compost,

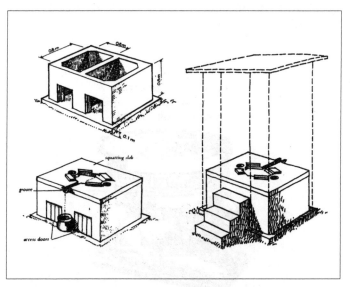

Kjell Torstensson. From *Sanitation without water* by Uno Winblad and Wen Kilama (Macmillan, 1985)

is removed from vault two, the lid is moved to vault one, and the family moves across.

The safe, odourless compost makes excellent fertilizer; according to the Ministry of Health, experiments in agricultural co-operatives show it can increase the yield of crops by 10-25%.

See also composting lavatories, earth-closets, India, Moule, pit latrines.

Vitreous china

Most lavatory pans are made of vitreous china, which became economically viable in the building boom after the Second World War. Before then the clay shape was made and fired to make glost; this was glazed, then fired again. This was an expensive process, and the glaze was always subject to crazing. The material was called biscuit-ware, either because it broke like a biscuit, or perhaps from the French *biscuit*, meaning 'twice cooked', or twice-fired.

No. 204
BAXENDALE'S REGISTERED
No. 48,570,
PEDESTAL LION CLOSET.

Height 16¼", basin 16¾" × 15"

Vitreous china is made from ball clay, china clay, silica, and fluxing agent. Its great advantage is that the clay body and the glaze body are compatible, which means that they can be fired together, because they both expand and contract by the same amount in the kiln. *See* how to make a loo.

The glaze is not strictly needed for hygiene, because in the kiln the clay vitrifies—turns to an impervious glassy solid—so the whole thickness of vitreous china is waterproof and stain-proof, and will not burn, rot, or rust. The surface cannot craze, and is inhospitable to bacteria.

W

Wash-down closets

The main rival to the wash-out closet (*see overleaf*), and a simple development of the hopper, is the wash-down closet. The flushing water, released from under the porcelain rim, cascades down all around the bowl and sweeps all before it through the *s-bend at the bottom—or at least that is the theory. In practice, the exact shape of the bowl and the arrangement and force of the flush sometimes prevent it from working as well as it should; by the time the water reaches the bottom it is flowing slowly, and the walls may stay smeared.

Also the faeces have a long way to fall, which probably causes more noise and splashing than in wash-out closets. Nevertheless the wash-down is now by far the most common lavatory in Britain; so in Darwinian terms it must be the fittest for its UK purpose.

Wash-out closets

Common today in Germany, France, and North America, the wash-out or flush-out closet is low and long, with a shallow pool of water at the back and a platform in front of it. Flushing produces an energetic jet of water from the back, which drives any offering out over the plateau and into the trap below, whence it is removed by the flow and in some cases by *siphonic action. A clear advantage of this design is that the faeces have only a short way to fall. This should mean less noise, and less splashing.

Disrespectful travellers have suggested that flush-out closets have a flat platform because the French and the Germans are obsessive about wanting to examine their stools. In practice this design allows a sharp undercutting surge of water cleanly to remove even sticky excrement more efficiently than in any wash-down design. Furthermore the wash-out closet was patented in Britain by George Jennings in 1852, which is probably well before it appeared in Germany or France.

Water-closets

The *OED* says a water-closet is 'a closet or small room fitted up to serve as a privy, and furnished with water supply to flush the pan and discharge its contents into a waste-pipe below. Often abbreviated W.C.' The term has been in use since 1755.

People seem to have been flushing lavatories with water for at least 4,000 years (*see* history), and the *Romans had flushing latrines in England 2,000 years ago—although technically their latrines did not have separate pans—so it seems foolish to claim that the water-closet was invented by one particular person.

A self-contained water-closet was made by Thomas Brightwell of the parish of St Martin in 1449, but we don't know much about it, except that it was flushed by rainwater, collected in a lead cistern; *see also* the Abbot of St Albans. For the earliest one we do know about—1596—*see* *Harington.

The first patent for a water-closet was taken out by Alexander *Cumming in 1775, and his sliding-valve

THE "Beaufort" Pedestal Closet.

STRONG. CHEAP. RELIABLE.

COMBINING

WATER CLOSET, URINAL, AND SLOP CLOSET.

The Original Pedestal Wash-Down Closet.

The Original Pedestal Wash-Down Closet.

Complete as shown with white basin and trap, polished mahogany seat, white paper box, 2 gall. galvanised syphon cistern, galvanised brackets, ivory pull and brass chain £3 15 0

Galvanized Seat Brackets, 8/6 extra.

device was improved by Joseph *Bramah in 1778. *See also* Crapper.

Women's room (The)

Marilyn French's novel *The women's room* is one of the most famous novels of the Women's Liberation Movement. It begins:

> Mira was hiding in the ladies' room. She called it that, even though someone had scratched out the word ladies in the sign on the door, and written women's underneath. She called it that out of thirty-eight years of habit, and until she saw the cross-out on the door had never thought about it. 'Ladies' room' was a euphemism, she supposed …
>
> But here she was at the age of thirty-eight, huddled for safety in a toilet booth at the basement of Sever Hall … She was perched, fully clothed, on the edge of the open toilet seat, feeling stupid and helpless, and constantly looking at her watch.

Y

Yachts

Ocean-going craft have plenty of sea water for flushing and disposal, and do not want to carry sewage about in sloshing chemical bins. Most systems pump sea water into the lavatory and pump the sewage out into the sea, even though this is illegal close inshore. That does not stop people from doing it, however, and a hundred yachts moored up-river can mean a deadly early morning swim!

In order to install one of these lavatories you need two holes in your hull, fitted with seacocks (taps). The inlet seacock should be well below the waterline and if possible on the other side of the boat from the discharge seacock, or at least further forward; you do not want to pull in fresh sewage with every flush. The discharge seacock should also be below the waterline.

The Baby Blake

The Rolls-Royce of small-boat lavatories was the Baby Blake; all mahogany, porcelain, and brass, and built to last a lifetime. When you had finished (I have been told by a proud user) you pumped the large handle and watched the turd circle the bowl, align itself with the exit hole, and then stand upright like a torpedoed ship before vanishing. A second pump handle pulled in fresh sea water to flush the bowl. The Baby Blake had a waterline marked half-way up the bowl, and the idea was to fill it to the mark after flushing.

See also boats, submariners, Royal Navy.

Z

Zen and the art of excretion

In his manual of Zen training, *Selling water by the river*, Jiyu Kennett says there is a special small ceremony before using the lavatory; this verse should be recited three times:

Adoration to all the Buddhas.
Adoration to the limitless teaching.

Peace! Speak! Blaze! Up! Open!
To the glorious, peaceful one for whom there is no
   disaster
Whilst upon the water-closet, Hail!

Dogen Zenji's *Shobogenzo* devotes a whole chapter to
Senjo. Those practising outdoors must use a privy, and
for cleaning themselves arrange seven balls of sand into
two rows. Monks practising indoors must enter the
lavatory, or *tosu* from the left-hand side of the corridor,
with a towel folded in two on the left shoulder, and
purify the lavatory by snapping together three times
the thumb and index finger of the right hand. When
finished, hold the water bucket in the right hand, cup
water in the left, and wash the genitals and buttocks
three times.

Zero-gravity toilet

Early in the second part of Stanley Kubrick's wonderful
1968 film *2001, A Space Odyssey*, the hero Heywood
Floyd takes a shuttle trip to the Moon. He goes to the
lavatory, sits down, and then his eyes narrow and his
brow wrinkles as he looks across at the back of the
door. There hangs a notice—several hundred words of
detailed instructions—under the heading ZERO-GRAVITY
TOILET. A copy now hangs in the bathroom of Arthur C.
Clarke, who wrote the screenplay.

Bibliography

Alsop, Reese F., 'The audio catheter', *New England journal of medicine* 808, 1974.

Amis, P., 'Some domestic vessels of southern Britain: a social and technical analysis', *Journal of ceramic history*, No. 2, 1968.

Baden-Powell, Robert, *Scouting for boys*, The Scout Association (35th Edition), London, 1991.

Bennett, Alan, Cook, Peter, Miller, Jonathan, and Moore, Dudley, *The complete beyond the fringe*, Souvenir Press, London, 1963; Methuen, London, 1987.

Bonington, Chris, *Everest, south west face*, Hodder & Stoughton, London, 1973.

Bound, William H., and Atkinson, Robert I., 'Bacterial aerosol from water closets', *The Lancet* 1369, 1966.

Burgess, Anthony, *Inside Mr Enderby*, Heinemann, London, 1963; *Enderby outside*, Heinemann, London, 1968; *The clockwork testament*, or *Enderby's end*, Hart-Davis MacGibbon, London, 1974; *Enderby's dark lady*, Hutchinson, London, 1984.

Burkitt, Denis, *Don't forget the fibre in your diet*, Martin Dunitz, London, 1979.

Burkitt, D. P. and Trowell, H.C., *Refined carbohydrate foods and disease*, Academic Press, London, New York, San Francisco, 1975.

Cavanagh, Sue, and Ware, Vron, *At women's convenience*, Women's Design Service, London, 1990.

Chevallier, Gabriel, *Clochemerle*, translated from the French by Jocelyn Godefroi, Secker & Warburg, London, 1936; Mandarin, London, 1993.

Cleave, T.L., *The saccharine disease*, John Wright, Bristol, 1974.

Crow, James, *English Heritage book of housesteads*, Batsford, London, 1995.

Cruikshank, Dan, and Burton, Neil, *Life in the Georgian city*, Viking, London, 1990.

Dickson, Camilla, personal communication to author; information also appears in Knights, B.A. et al., *Journal of archaeological science* 10, 1983, pp. 139-52, 1983.

Don, G. Graham, 'Public conveniences in the London area', *The Medical Officer*, 8 December 1961.

Donno, Elizabeth Story, *Sir John Harington's A new discourse of a stale subject, called the metamorphosis of Ajax, a critical edition*, Routledge & Kegan Paul, London, 1962.

Ellis, Hamilton, *Railway carriages in the British Isles from 1830-1914*, George Allen & Unwin, London, 1965.

Ewen, Robert B., *An introduction to theories of personality* (4th Edition), Lawrence Erlbaum Associates, Hillside NJ, Hove and London, 1993.

Franceys, R., Pickford J., and Reed, R., *A guide to the development of on-site sanitation*, WHO Geneva, 1992.

French, Marilyn, *The women's room*, Sphere Books, London, 1978.

Gilbaugh, James H., and Fuchs, Peter C., 'The gonococcus and the toilet seat', *New England Journal of Medicine* 301, 91-3, 1979.

Girouard, Mark, *Life in the English country house*, Yale University Press, New Haven and London, 1978.

Harper, Peter, and Thorpe, Dave, *Fertile waste*, The Centre for Alternative Technology, Machynlleth, 1994.

Harris, Mollie, and Chapman, Sue, *Cotswold privies*, Chatto & Windus, London, 1984.

Heaton, K.W., *Understanding your bowels*, Family doctor publications, London, 1995—available in large chemists' shops.

Hellyer, S. Stevens, *The plumber and sanitary houses*, a practical treatise *on the* principles *of* internal plumbing work, *or the* best *means for* effectually *excluding* noxious gases *from our houses*, Batsford, London, 1877.

Hughes, Victoria, *Ladies mile*, Abson Books, Bristol, 1977.

Jackson, R., *Doctors and diseases in the Roman Empire*, British Museum Press, 1988.

Joseph, Franz, *Star fleet technical manual*, Titan Books, London, 1991.

Kilroy, Roger, *The compleat loo, a lavatorial miscellany*, Victor Gollancz, London, 1984.

Kimmage, Paul, *A rough ride*, Stanley Paul, London, 1990.

Kunkel, Paul, *How to toilet-train your cat*, Workman Publishing, New York, 1991.

Lambton, Lucinda, *Temples of convenience*, The Gordon Fraser Gallery, London and Bedford, 1978.

Lambton, Lucinda, *Chambers of delight*, The Gordon Fraser Gallery, London and Bedford, 1983.

Lambton, Lucinda, *Temples of convenience and chambers of delight*, Tempus, Stroud, 2007.

Leach, Penelope, *Babyhood*, Pelican, London 1974, (2nd Edition) 1983.

Lovelock, J.E., *Gaia, a new look at life on Earth*, Oxford University Press, 1979.

McNab, Andy, *Bravo two zero*, Bantam Press, London, 1993.

Markham, Len, *Yorkshire privies*, Countryside Books, Newbury, 1996.

Meyer, Kathleen, *How to shit in the woods*, Ten Speed Press, California, 1989.

Middlemist, R. Dennis, Knowles, Eric S., and Matter, Charles F., 'Personal space invasions in the lavatory: suggestive evidence for arousal', *Journal of personality and social psychology* 33, No. 5, 1976, pp. 541-6.

Murphy, Shirley Forster, *Our homes, and how to make them healthy*, Cassell & Co, London, 1885.

Palmer, Roy, *The water closet, a new history*, David & Charles, Newton Abbot, 1973.

Pudney, John, *The smallest room*, Michael Joseph, London, 1954.

Reyburn, Wallace, *Flushed with pride, the story of Thomas Crapper*, Macdonald, London, 1969; Pavilion Books, London, 1989.

Reynolds, Reginald, *Cleanliness and godliness*, George Allen & Unwin, London, 1943.

Rogers, S.A.B., *Four acres and a donkey, ordinary lives*, No. 3, ed. Clive Murphy, Dennis Dobson, London, 1979.

Sale, Charles, *The specialist*, Specialist Publishing Company, St Louis, Minnesota, 1929; Putnam & Co, London, 1930.

Sweeney, W.B. et al., 'The constipated serviceman', *Military medicine*, August 1993.

Teak, T. Pridgin, *Dangers to health*, J. & A. Churchill, London; (2nd Edition) Charles Goodall, Leeds, 1879.

Trevelyan, G.M., *English social history*, Longman, London, 1944.

Turner, Jean, *East Anglian privies*, Countryside Books, Newbury, 1996.

Waugh, Evelyn, *Men at arms* (First of the *Sword of honour* trilogy), Chapman & Hall, London, 1952; Penguin, London, 1964.

Wheeler, Mortimer, *Roman art and architecture*, Thames & Hudson, London, 1964.

Winblad, Uno and Kilama, Wen, *Sanitation without water*, Macmillan, London, 1985.

Wolfe, Tom, *The right stuff*, Jonathan Cape, London, 1979.

Wright, Lawrence, *Clean and decent*, Routledge & Kegan Paul, London, 1960.

Index

National College of Art & Design
LIBRARY
Ph: 01 636 4357

Books should be returned on or before the last date shown above. Books can be
renewed on-line (www.ncad.ie) or by phone (01-6364357). Fines will be charged for overdue books.